A NEIGHBOR'S PRIMER TO ORGANIZING, ADVOCACY, AND THE URGENCY OF COMMUNITY

A Neighbor's Primer to Organizing, Advocacy, and the Urgency of Community

Armando Moritz-Chapelliquen

ISBN: 979-8-9948564-0-6
Library of Congress Control Number: 2026911513

Printed in the United States of America
First Printing, 2026

Editing by Melinda Masson

Astyanax Press
AstyanaxBooks.com

Visit the author's website at www.armando-mc.com

For Miles: May the world you inherit be one where these
lessons are unnecessary

Contents

ILLUSTRATIONS

PREFACE

If you are reading this, you are likely experiencing one of the following sentiments: worry about the future, desire to do something about it, or eagerness to learn the skills necessary to make change possible in your neighborhood. Perhaps you feel a combination of these; perhaps all three. Since the rise of the nonprofit sector, the work of being an "organizer" or "advocate" has become professionalized. While the recognition of organizing and advocacy as real work deserving of pay is largely a positive development, the fact that this vital social role became a career path implicitly made the work less accessible. As a result, organizing and advocacy work may be seen as too complicated, too time-consuming, and too hard for a "regular" person.

While organizing and advocacy work absolutely requires specialized skills to be effective, the reality is that a lot of successful organizing and advocacy work has been and continues to be done by untrained and unpaid individuals—in other words, "regular" people like you and your neighbors. Anyone willing to learn can develop these skills over time. What cannot be taught is the desire to improve our communities, which helps to fuel and sustain this work. We all live in the same world, but not all of us are worried about the future, eager to do something about it, or willing to learn the skills necessary to make change possible. Anxiety, empathy, and curiosity cannot be taught. If you wish to develop the skills to act on these feelings, however, I hope the following text will be helpful in aiding you to make this world a better place.

In the popular imagination, the organizer or advocate is the clipboard-carrying, bullhorn-blasting, charismatic leader of a mass of people. The popular imagination is wrong. Organizers and advocates are facilitators of change. As will be discussed in Chapter 4, facilitators are not necessarily the loudest or the most charismatic people in a meeting or event. They are mature enough to be engaging with others, strategic enough to know when to lean in or lean back, and collaborative enough to appreciate that getting big things done requires big groups of people working together. All of these factors apply to organizers and advocates as well. If this less fantastical bar excites you, you're in the right place.

I offer this perspective because for the better part of my professional career, I've been in organizing and advocacy spaces. And while I have participated in plenty of marches, rallies, and public actions, I've come to appreciate the less glamorous and more frustrating elements of social justice work: interpreting people's handwriting to build out contact lists of potentially interested neighbors, overcoming social awkwardness to knock on neighbors' doors and get them politically involved against the redevelopment of an old industrial site, trying (and sometimes failing) to convince your allies to take a strategic position instead of going for the quick catharsis of spectacle. I don't claim to be the best organizer or advocate, but I've been around enough great ones to learn lessons that I think are worth sharing.

Being an **organizer** means *working with* an impacted class of people to achieve improvements in their material conditions. Being an **advocate** means *working on behalf of* an impacted class of people to achieve improvements in their material conditions. You do not need to be at the front of the room or at the vanguard of a march to do either of these things. All that matters is your engagement with the impacted class of people.

At the time of this writing, that impacted class of people is getting larger and larger. The fundamental pillars of American civil society are being eroded by those who swore to uphold them, causing fear, panic, and a gradual decline in the social, political, and economic order. It is easy to feel overwhelmed, but paralysis rooted in shock only benefits the oppressor. The work of addressing the countless injustices being committed, reviving the values we claimed to represent, and advancing a vision of a free and just society is the work not of a single person, but of communities working together.

Much has been written about the decline of community and civic virtue over the second half of the twentieth century.[1] Rather than attempt to validate or challenge the reasons for that decline, we should address it. We must prioritize the reinvigoration of community and civic virtue in order to achieve three vital objectives:

1. Form a broad movement that can effectively counter the rising tide of authoritarianism.
2. Create the physical, social, emotional, and mental space necessary for envisioning a better future.
3. Remain engaged and sane in a time of rolling crises.

These goals are not mutually exclusive. Rather, they all reiterate a basic ideal of people looking out for one another: Individuals can check on their neighbors; neighborhoods can respond collectively to shared crises to soften the blow on the most heavily impacted; associations can form to create space for people to interact and share their priorities for the future. Not every community relationship needs to be a bond of eternal friendship, but engaging with one another on a human level, offline and in-person, is a necessary condition for applying any of the skills or theories in the subsequent chapters. Perhaps the biggest obstacle to being an organizer or advocate in the digital age is lacking the wherewithal and confidence to make such interactions happen. While this text does not have a chapter on confidence, it provides some information that will hopefully be useful in those interactions.

All of this being said, the role of an organizer or advocate is incredibly accessible. While organizing and advocacy work (and their associated skill sets) can generally be used in a positive or negative context, my hope is that you use the skills learned here to advance goals associated with or derivative of the following principles:

- Our coalitions must reflect the diversity of our communities.
- Every person has inherent dignity and power.
- This work is measured by the material improvement we bring to people's lives.

This book is broken up into three main parts, with review questions inviting further reflection after each chapter. Part I outlines the language, theory, and concepts that underpin much of community-oriented social justice work. Through this section, you will be introduced to some of the basic terminology of organizing and advocacy spaces. You will come to interrogate and reflect on your own understanding of power, the types of power you have, and how to discuss these issues of power within your communities. Part II explores some of the central skills for organizers and advocates looking to mobilize their communities. While they are not the only skills necessary to enact social change, any good organizer or advocate should at least appreciate the importance of meeting facilitation, public speaking, and power mapping. Part III closes the book with final reflections on community building and preparing yourself for the ordeals of our present moment. The appendix offers templates, checklists, and questions to consider when applying the skills presented throughout this text. This book is offered as a way to self-reflect and initiate discussions with others who are concerned about the increasing violence against our neighbors and the dismantling of our contemporary political, economic, and social order. The lessons I'll share are rooted in conversations, campaigns, and coalitions that succeeded, failed, and stalled at the local, state, and national level. Where there is more to be said, consider it an invitation to advance answers in your own community. This is my attempt to begin a conversation to strengthen our communities; I encourage you to reflect on these lessons, apply them in your community, and carry the conversation forward.

NOTES

[1]See, for example, Robert Putnam's *Bowling Alone: The Collapse and Revival of American Community* (Simon & Schuster, 2000).

ACKNOWLEDGMENTS

Writing this text has been an exercise in self-actualization, and I want to thank those who brought me closer to achieving what is now in your hands: a primer to organizing, advocacy, and the urgency of community.

To KP, Lauren, and Rohit, thank you for your patience and insights as you read multiple initial drafts.

To Colleen, Kendra, Cody, Trina, and Josie, thank you for your commitment to take on the necessary work of fighting for our neighborhoods, whether through opposition to the mega warehouse, interventions to meet the emotional and economic needs of area families, or willingness to put your bodies on the line.

To Henry, Michele, Rich, Michelle, and Jen, thank you for showing my family how such an aspirational vision of community can be realized today.

To Elizabeth, Andrea, Destiny, Lorena, David, Sarah, Marcus, Jamie, Koa, Caroline, Jackie, Daniel, Shauntrice, Sakuri, Jessica, Leilah, Tina, Julianne, Ephraim, Sandylane, and George, thank you for uplifting the local voices of community in the work of national endeavors.

To Emily, Lauren, Israh, Melanie, Barika, Krystal, Susanna, Leah, Megan, Farouk, Kevin, Andy, Jaqi, Jason, Ben, Ted, Jess, Patty, Antoinette, Tiffany, Ruben, Jaime, Patrick, Gary, Fara, Khristina, Arash, and Bernie—organizers, advocates, and philosophers I've had the privilege to learn from and aspire toward—thank you for planting the seeds over months, years, and decades that have emerged in the branches of this text.

To Kimberly, to Ryan, and to Joe, thank you for living lives with the conviction of achieving a better world.

To my parents, thank you for seeing the value of raising and supporting the next generation to be better than your own.

Most importantly, I thank Ada, whose relentless belief in the ideas I hold and words I write made all this possible. You continue to be, as ever, my muse.

THEORETICAL FOUNDATIONS

Power, properly understood, is the ability to achieve purpose. It is the strength required to bring about social, political, or economic changes.

—DR. MARTIN LUTHER KING JR.

Organizing, advocacy, and community-building work requires self-reflection, adaptation, and curiosity. Self-reflection brings mindfulness about yourself and your relationships. Adaptation creates opportunity to make your actions your own. Curiosity fuels both as you act upon your desire to change the world.

These elements together represent the theoretical foundation for the organizing, advocacy, and community-building work explored in this text. From this foundation, we will build an understanding of social justice terminology and begin to unpack the complexities around power. While the terminology and specifically the term *power* appear frequently in popular discourse, the following chapters are presented without consideration for their use in legacy or social media. Having heard these words on the news or online, you may need to unlearn some of the biases commonly associated with them. That unlearning should not be arbitrary, and the concepts to follow should not be adopted without scrutiny. Self-reflection is not the same as self-doubt; a curious mind will question past knowledge as well as new information. After all, the second foundational concept is *adaptation*, not wholesale adoption.

While you should reflect on what you learn or unlearn, how you adapt the following concepts to your own circumstances will demonstrate your associated level of mastery. This adaptation is not meant to be a solitary activity; it is one that is applied to your surroundings and in relation to other people. Application of theory and learning from that experience is the core of **praxis**. While there are skills to physically practice as an organizer or advocate (to be explored in Part II), theoretical practice is only truly accomplished through dialogue with allies, opponents, and those who are still uncertain where they stand. Through this application, your understanding will be tested, developed, and refined. At the same time, the understanding of those you engage with will be similarly tested, developed, and refined. While the victories or losses of these theoretical practices—conversations—are often intangible aside from our own sense of satisfaction or frustration, they are the seeds from which change at the local, statewide, and national level can bloom. It is for this reason that we must be mindful of the theory we seed in our minds and spread to others.

1

The Language of Social Justice

Effectively working in any field requires an understanding of that field's terminology. For people eager to get into community-oriented social justice work, that is the space of organizers and advocates. As with any space, particular terms are used to express and describe specific concepts. In the absence of curiosity, those terms can get thrown around without careful consideration of the concepts they represent, diluting their original meaning and making discussions more confusing than productive. Eventually, these discussions become meaningless, a free-for-all of keywords detached from meaning or direct experience. To avoid this pitfall, it is important to take the time to interrogate and understand several key terms in social justice spaces. While none of the terms themselves are particularly complicated, dissecting them will create a firm language base for future organizing, advocacy, and community-building work.

Community

Community is the totality of positive and negative relationships within a given area. Communities are rooted in physical spaces: the neighbors in your building or on your block, the parents you see when walking your kids to school, and the business owners and workers you engage with in your day-to-day affairs. It can also be the noisy neighbors, the littering passersby, or the cantankerous elders who don't like seeing change. The sum of these interactions creates community. Communities can be welcoming or insular, vibrant or stale, and growing or shrinking. The scale of community can also vary widely, from the floor of a building to multiple municipal blocks. Communities are likely to be heterogeneous, meaning that they have a mix of economic classes, ages, ethnicities, national origins, and several other demographic identifiers. This diversity of backgrounds and experiences is in some ways inherent to communities, because a healthy community is one where people from different backgrounds live together, see the humanity in each other, and, in the best cases, support one another. And while they will not always agree, they are capable of resolving or addressing disputes while recognizing the humanity in each other.

Since the beginning of the internet, the term *community* has taken on a dramatically new meaning, coming to encapsulate any assemblage of people who share a common identity, such as appreciation for a team, hobby, political affiliation, or demographic identifier. I do not wish to minimize the importance of finding like-minded individuals who share a common identity through the internet and specifically social media, but such uniformity and commonality do not typically exist in day-to-day interactions. The best example for the heterogeneity of communities can be found in those places outside of home and work where individuals gather: parks, libraries, schools, Laundromats, and so on. These locations, termed by sociologists as *third places*[1], can demonstrate the diversity of individuals and families in an area.

While we could attempt to limit our interactions to only those who share in a preferred common identity, the reality is that we are all very different from one another and we should—within reason—accept that. An obvious caveat here is that the inherent dignity of every person is non-negotiable; bigotry in its various forms is antithetical to the concept of a vibrant community. The profoundly human value of empathy is necessary to engaging honestly and earnestly with other people, whether we like them or not. We all physically reside in neighborhoods and municipalities, urban cores and rural areas, but without engagement with the other people in these areas, we lack community.

Organizing and Advocacy

Organizing is the act of *working alongside other impacted people* to achieve a shared goal. That goal can be the passage of a law, the changing of an existing policy, or the meeting of a particular demand. Notable examples of community members organizing include

- Elizabeth Cady Stanton for women's rights,
- Marsha P. Johnson for trans rights, and
- Starbucks workers unionizing for better wages and working conditions.

Advocacy is the act of *working on behalf of other impacted people* to achieve a shared goal. The critical distinction between these two concepts is an individual's relationship to other people. Someone doing organizing work does not work alone. Someone doing advocacy work can.

While the actions themselves can be mutually exclusive, there are plenty of cases of organizing becoming advocacy and vice versa. For example, someone's individual advocacy can evolve into organizing work if others choose to get directly involved. The opposite is also true: A large group's organizing efforts can become advocacy work if members disengage and leave key decisions in the hands of a single person or steering committee. *The involvement of others and their level of engagement is the key distinction.* However, the issue of engagement only creates more issues: How engaged is engaged enough for efforts to be organizing instead of advocacy? Who determines the appropriate level of engagement? Because the right answers largely depend upon the people being organized or doing the advocacy, these and other questions are better addressed using real-life cases rather than hypothetical situations.

Strategy and Tactics

Strategy is a planned series of interconnected actions that work toward the achievement of a goal. Strategies can be complicated and winding, seemingly one step backward yet three steps forward. At its core, a strategy is a plan. That plan can be confusing, but confusion may be necessary for facilitating the achievement of a goal. Being strategic, therefore, means to think about—and plan around—the interconnected actions that work toward achieving a goal.

Tactics are the individual acts that make up a strategy. Tactics commonly associated with organizing and advocacy include door-knocking, in-person meetings, virtual meetings, posting flyers, and using social media. Individually, these tactics may not lead to an intended outcome or be particularly successful. Combined and structured around an outreach strategy, however, the tactics may be much more effective. Because individuals can get better at door-knocking, hosting in-person meetings, or engaging on social media, being tactical simply means employing a particular skill set that is valuable in the context of a broader strategy.

Campaigns

Campaigns are a series of activities that work in service to a goal. Distinct from strategies, the activities supporting a campaign do not need to be connected by any internal logic. In other words, there does not need to be an overarching plan. Any series of activities in service of a goal can be considered a campaign, even if those activities undermine one another. Clearly, the bar for what classifies as a campaign is not especially high.

Given this relatively straightforward definition, it might be more useful to define what makes an effective or "good" campaign. As you may guess, an *effective campaign* comprises a well-executed strategy: The series of activities that work in service of a goal should be an implemented sequence of planned actions.

Politics

Politics permeates every aspect of our lives—in practical and emotional ways. Politics in its most basic and fundamental form involves people exerting power over their surroundings. To unpack that, we can refer to Dr. Martin Luther King Jr.'s framing of power as "the ability to achieve purpose."[2] Therefore, **politics** involves people exerting the ability to achieve purpose over their surroundings. That "purpose" could be their own bodily autonomy, the future of a vacant site in their neighborhood, or the rights of another person in their community. And while "surroundings" can be broadly interpreted to include national and state politics, the most immediate surroundings are your own neighborhood.

As these examples illustrate, to say politics is just about power misses some important context: power exerted by whom, over whom, and over what? Because people do not exist in a vacuum, these questions of power inevitably play out between individuals and groups at international, national, statewide, and local levels. If this seems overwhelming, that is because it is. For people to want to ignore these dynamics—to "not make things political"—is understandable; however, when people say they don't want to make things political, they are really saying one of the following:

- I don't want to acknowledge how power is actively being used in my community.

- I don't want to acknowledge my own power and how it impacts my perception of my community.
- I don't look at things through a lens that examines power and how it is being actively used in my community.

Being political simply means identifying, examining, and questioning the nature of power relationships in a given space. As these dynamics exist in almost every space, choosing not to be political means not fully perceiving your own surroundings, whether because of naivete or willful ignorance. In this context, being a political organizer or political advocate means taking the next step after questioning those relationships: You are working—with others or alone—to change the power dynamics. For the purposes of our discussion, those changes will happen in communities.

Political Education

Political education entails learning about power and its use in communities and between people. Political education can involve learning how laws formally get passed, how laws actually get passed, who are the elected officials in your town council, what books are being removed from school libraries (and by whom), or why it takes so long for potholes to get fixed. Political education yields insights about power, who has it, and how it is used in a given area.

Popular Education

Popular education is less a stand-alone subject area and more a methodology of learning. *What* one learns is not the same as *how* one learns. That's the distinction between political education and popular education. **Popular education** is a way of learning that allows for an individual to actively and collaboratively learn as part of a group.

Consider the following two scenarios in which a group of people are trying to understand how a law will impact their lives:

In one scenario, a person in the group stands up, says that they're a lawyer or policy expert, and proceeds to explain how the law will impact everyone in the group. This person goes on to cite research, their own lived experience, and statistics that effectively support their explanation of the law, ensuring every person in the group understands the policy impacts.

In another scenario, a person stands up and asks everyone to share how they think the law will impact them. Each person shares their impressions, with some citing research, lived experiences, and statistics. Through this process, it becomes clear that each person is experiencing this law differently, whether because of their age, gender, economic class, or national origin. While not every member of the group may fully understand the law's impacts, and some may need to conduct additional research or follow-up, the act of learning has occurred through the process of collective reflection and dialogue.

Although both scenarios represent political education, only the second can be considered popular education. Why? Because it is participatory: It meaningfully engages the learners in a way that respects their lived experiences. By contrast, the first scenario can be interpreted as the "'banking' concept of education,"[3] where an expert or teacher "deposits" knowledge or insights into the "receptacles," the students. In such an educational setup, the teacher holds the knowledge that the students receive. Learning is, in this configuration, a one-way transaction.

Popular education can and likely should occur more slowly, because the goal is not to convey information as quickly as possible from one mind to another, but to effectively examine shared information as collectively as possible. In the second scenario, the participation of all group members through dialogue empowers each individual to uncover and understand the new information provided by their fellow "students." Some people learn through conversation, others through pictures, and others still through text. Particularly for popular education, the focus is on the people learning as opposed to the knowledge being learned.

Becoming Fluent
in the Language of Social Justice

As with any subject, speaking with confidence requires a deep understanding of the topics you discuss. For any individual doing any kind of campaign, whether collective organizing or solitary advocacy, the ability to clearly communicate the goals of their efforts and the methods utilized to reach those goals is crucial. Politics focuses on power wielded by and upon people. If you want to change anything about the current state of politics, you will need people to go along with you, and for that to happen, you need to be able to converse with them in a shared language.

Because of the pervasiveness and polarization of politics in everyday life, anyone you speak with is likely to have preconceived notions about many of the terms defined in this chapter. Those notions might align with your definitions, and they might not. Still, even if others disagree with your definitions, your most strategic next step is to try to understand their perspective. In the spirit of popular education, you can point out the power relationships we are all experiencing, you can challenge those relationships, and you can do so in a way that respects the expertise of others' lived experiences. Being fluent in the language of social justice is not a matter of memorizing these terms and their definitions; it means having the patience and capacity to discuss these terms with others. In the process, you're bound to find like-minded individuals who are willing to work with you. It all comes back to dialogue: talking *with*, not talking *to*; working *with*, not working *for*.

Review Questions

- Where does community "happen" in your area?
- How can you practice using the terms defined in this chapter in a low-stress environment? Who can you talk to about them?
- What skills do you have, and how do they align with any of these terms? Do you see yourself working in collaboration like an organizer? Analyzing the necessary steps to accomplish a campaign? Learning alongside others through popular education?
- Given the increasingly politicized nature of day-to-day life, how do you think you can approach conversations with those who "don't want to make things political"?
- Where does political education happen in your community?

NOTES

[1] Ray Oldenburg, *The Great Good Place: Cafes, Coffee Shops, Bookstores, Bars, Hair Salons, and Other Hangouts at the Heart of a Community*, 2nd ed. (Berkshire Publishing Group, 2023).

[2] Quoted in Roy Wilson, "Dr. King's Words About Nonviolence and Power," Martin Luther King Jr. Freedom Center, February 3, 2024, https://mlkfreedomcenter.org/dr-kings-words-about-nonviolence-power/.

[3] Paulo Freire, *Pedagogy of the Oppressed*, 30th anniversary ed., trans. Myra Bergman Ramos (Continuum, 2005), 72.

2

Forms of Power

Any meaningful social justice conversation either begins or inevitably reaches a discussion on power—who has it, how it is used, and how it can be better wielded. Thankfully, as featured in Part I, Dr. Martin Luther King Jr. provided a simple definition of **power**: "the ability to achieve purpose" and "the strength required to bring about social, political, or economic changes."[1] With this definition in mind, we can now consider two forms of power that manifest in all communities, and recognize that all people within these communities have some mixture of the two. While power generally is understood in its aggregate—what we'll refer to as *total power*—it is important to differentiate between formal and informal power as each functions very differently (see Figure 1 for examples).

Formal Power

Formal power is relatively straightforward: It is the power automatically given or conferred to an individual or group as a matter of professional, economic, or political position. For example, elected and unelected government officials occupy a position by which they are given certain powers. Such government positions are defined and established as a matter of law, whether in a constitution, a charter, or bylaws. The individuals who occupy these positions inherit their formal power from their predecessors and eventually pass them on to a successor. The position, not the individual, holds the power. This distinction is significant, as it emphasizes the impersonal nature of formal power: An elected official who fails to win reelection loses their formal power because they have lost a *position.*

While government officials most easily exemplify formal power, several other cases are equally relevant to building community power: Upon hiring staff and formalizing a business, employers and employees have certain formal powers as defined by law. Citizens, or at least those registered to vote, have the formal power to express approval or disapproval of their elected officials through elections. Academics and credentialed experts have formal power by virtue of their title (e.g., *doctor* or *lawyer*). In all of these cases, the power is conferred on positions, not individuals. Similarly, these types of formal power—to discipline staff or form a union, to vote, and to inform matters within your sphere of expertise—can all be taken away.

Across the spectrum of formal power, there is a singular thread: the official recognition and designation of power through an established authority. In the case of politics, formal power often depends upon the adherence to law in order to remain relevant. As the law is strengthened, so too are the mechanisms and authorities that grant formal power. As the law is weakened, so too are the same mechanisms and authorities. In short, formal power depends on the strength of the institutions that originally defined it. For example, the formal power of a town council depends on the council's charter or code, the state constitution that granted powers to the local government, and the federal government's laws that granted powers to the states.

Although formal power, as noted, may be easiest to understand in the context of government officials, in reality all formal power is somewhat fickle. A certified professional in a field may need to regularly maintain their certification through ongoing courses. An employee may need to demonstrate some basic competencies to maintain their position or advance in their job. A voter will need to reregister to vote if they move or wish to change their party affiliation. In short, formal power often requires some level of maintenance in order to be kept by an individual. Reelection to a governmental position is the most obvious case, but hardly the only one. While individuals may utilize formal power in their own interest, the power inherently belongs not to them, but to the position they occupy.

It is important to emphasize that formal power and "rights" are closely related but not interchangeable. *Rights* refer to the legally defined power of an individual, a group, or an institution. In other words, it is a type of formal power. For example, the right to vote is a formal power granted to US citizens, though it took much of this nation's history for that formal power to be extended to all citizens. Even now, this right is under attack in several jurisdictions. As previously indicated, formal power may be granted based on an individual's vocation, professional affiliation, or certifications. What all types of formal power have in common is that they can, unfortunately, be taken away.

Informal Power

Where formal power depends on position, **informal power** is gained through camaraderie, friendship, partnership, and shared experiences—in other words, as a result of interpersonal relationships. As the name suggests, informal power is not typically defined or established in a formal document. To understand informal power, consider a well-known resident in your neighborhood. They may have helped you in a time of need, their children may play with your children on the weekends, or perhaps they are always willing to share information about local events. None of these characteristics directly give this individual power, but the strength of their relationships grants them a level of credibility, trust, and clout. Often identified as the "unofficial mayor" or "community leader," they are reliable and trustworthy, and their perspective can greatly shape public opinion. This is their informal power.

Unlike formal power, informal power is entirely connected to the individual. As with relationships themselves, informal power is not easily transferable from one person to another. Where formal power is explicitly set and defined, informal power is continuously changing and amorphous. Because informal power is so contingent upon relationships and trust, it can expand and contract more quickly and variously than formal power. Moreover, while informal power does not necessarily require renewal in the way formal power does, maintaining a given level of informal power requires maintaining healthy relationships.

Although formal power may be easier to quantify, an individual with significant informal power has the potential to be more influential in enacting change. For example, a well-regarded neighborhood parent could sway a local election in ways a senator could not. Informal power may be harder to recognize by an outsider to a community but will be obvious to any well-connected individuals or longtime residents.

Because informal power is not explicitly grounded in any formal constitution or charter, its emergence can be difficult to predict. In the aforementioned scenario, the parent's ability to wield more influence than a senator may have nothing to do with electoral politics or the legislative accomplishments of the senator (our stand-in for formal power). The parent's influence could be rooted in electoral politics or more simply tied to the trust placed in them by several neighbors. In some ways, the source of the influence is irrelevant to its application: Exercising informal power can have ramifications for the entire community.

In the case of building community power, the foundational power for organizers and advocates is almost always relational. As such, building any kind of meaningful relationships with others can eventually yield significant informal power. To this point, sometimes the

Formal Power: Public School
- The power dynamic is rooted in law and formal regulations against truancy.
- Any preexisting relationship is unnecessary; parents do not typically choose their child's teacher or classroom.
- State laws apply to parents, who act by sending their kids to school.

Formal Power: Professional Certification
- Credentialed professionals are expected to remain in good standing by the professional association.
- Personal relationships are irrelevant.
- Certification or a professional association's charge is applied to individuals, who act by remaining in good standing.

Informal Power: Neighbor Babysitting Your Kids
- The power dynamic is likely rooted in your relationship with your neighbor.
- The relationship lacks a contract or formally written agreement.
- Your informal duty as a parent is applied to your neighbor, who acts by taking care of your kids.

Figure 1. Three Examples of Formal and Informal Power

most effective way to build informal power with a group of people is to continue to be present. Because trust and camaraderie can lead to any number of different kinds of relationships, informal power can be developed in countless ways. Regardless, regularly showing up can be the first step in establishing a relationship with people and, ultimately, developing informal power.

Total Power

Total power is the sum of the formal and informal power any one person or entity holds. A distinct understanding of both forms is important because they can be conflated. To illustrate this point, consider the following scenario:

Two individuals in the same municipality are elected to their town council. Their terms of office begin on the same day. Both officials want to see their town's pool repaired and replaced. Official A, upon studying the budget, concludes the funding available is insufficient to repair the pool. Official B also studies the budget but, after reaching the same conclusion, starts a dialogue with neighboring municipalities to see how they attract funding from public and private sources.

In this scenario, Official B has more total power than Official A. While both have the same formal powers, Official B's relationship-building through outreach to neighboring communities gives them more informal power. Without understanding the distinction between formal and informal power, someone may simply conclude that Official B is a better town councilor than Official A. None of Official B's actions, however, are explicitly connected to the town councilor position. Official B may be using their position to build relationships with neighboring municipalities, but those relationships will belong to Official B, not to the position of town councilor. When Official B's term expires, assuming they maintained a good relationship with these neighboring municipalities, those relationships will follow them to their next role, whether in the government, nonprofit, or private sector. The only way the relationships would translate to the rest of the town council would be if Official B facilitated that transfer of relationships and, therefore, of informal power.

The same rules apply to "regular" people. Consider two individuals living in the same neighborhood. Both are US citizens, granting them equivalent formal powers, including the right to form a union. They each work the same job at the same company and receive the same amount of pay. While they agree that they should be paid more, only the first individual begins talking to coworkers about starting a union. Assuming these conversations go well, the individual who started them will have more informal power than the individual who agreed but did not act.

Of course, additional factors can alter who is more powerful in either scenario. In the first scenario, Official A may have a strong relationship with the local school district. In the second, the compliant employee may be more trusted by their peers than the aspiring labor organizer. These and other factors can influence who has more total power, but as the examples illustrate, those factors will often be on the side of informal power. This is partly because of informal power's generally amorphous nature. Another reason is that if an individual figured out a unique way to utilize their formal power, that application of formal power would be available to every other person in the same position. In other words, an individual's innovative use of formal power benefits every person with that formal power, not just themselves. An individual's innovative use of formal power would not change the fact that the power does not technically belong to them, but belongs to the position they occupy, be it citizen, employee, or legislator.

Translating Power

An individual or group's total power will ultimately influence how effectively they enact the changes or agenda they wish to see. As their formal or informal power grows, a ceiling eventually may be reached in either category, leading the individual to consider translating their formal power into informal power, or vice versa. This translation is common enough in both directions that tropes about politicians can provide an adequate illustration:

Informal to Formal Power

An individual is a dedicated member of their community, volunteering with regional groups, staying connected with their neighbors, and being generally "plugged in" to local happenings. Recognizing their deep well of informal power, they see things going the wrong way in their community and decide to run for office to address these challenges directly. Because of their personal network being mobilized as volunteers, supporters, and financial contributors, they handily win their election and gain a seat in local government. Once they reach office, however, they get wrapped up in the broader bureaucracy and fail to deliver on the changes they originally sought. As a result, the personal relationships that propelled them to gain formal power suffer, and the vast informal power they once held begins to decline, leaving them largely dependent on the formal power of their elected office to have influence both in government and in their wider community.

Formal to Informal Power

On the flip side, consider a politician who has been in office for decades. They have come to understand the bureaucracy of government like the back of their hand. They have written and passed laws in friendly and hostile legislative environments. Over their years of public service, they have developed relationships with their peers in various agencies, departments, and political parties. Realizing they are tired of doing all this work (and perhaps detecting a difficult primary in the next election cycle), they decide to announce their retirement, then go on to join a lobbying firm, leveraging the skills and understanding of government they honed as an elected official and translating them into informal power. In this new role, the retired politician's day-to-day work is built entirely on the knowledge they developed while wielding formal power. The politician-turned-lobbyist will no longer sponsor legislation, but their experiences in government will ensure that they continue to influence the work of that body for years to come.

In the first scenario, the translation of informal to formal power led to a decline in the politician's total power. In the second, where formal power was translated into informal power, the politician's total power remained consistent, if not increased. While neither scenario is a foregone conclusion, the important takeaway is that translating formal or informal power can result in a net loss, net gain, or net neutral change to an individual's total power. As a result, it is important to recognize the opportunities and potential challenges involved with translating your informal power to formal power, or vice versa.

Of course, in various cases an individual's total power can increase without a loss of either formal power or informal power. Elected officials can gain or lose popularity (informal power) throughout their term. Successful advocacy groups can gain rights and protections (formal power) throughout a campaign. If you are interested in doing this work for an extended period, it is important to consider when and how your power and the power of your allies can shift. Sometimes translating power from one form to another is necessary; other times it is critical for your forms of power to remain as consistent as possible.

How Forms of Power Inform Community-Building Work

Any person focused on addressing social inequities should understand what kind of power they have and what kind of power they need. As with individuals, groups have their own mix of formal and informal power. By understanding the nature of their formal and informal power, they can more strategically leverage either type in a campaign for change. Strong relationships can lead to new rights and protections. New rights and protections can be leveraged to strengthen relationships. A virtuous cycle can form. For someone only starting out in community-building work, the first sources of power to tap are likely to be informal, but leveraging this power into tangible improvements in your neighbors' and allies' day-to-day lives can result in more informal and, eventually, formal power. As someone committed to advancing a cause, it is critical that you interrogate your own forms of power. Do you have an advanced degree? Are you well connected in your area? Is your job relevant to the community-oriented efforts you are driving? Sustainable organizing and advocacy efforts require a mix of formal and informal power. Because everyone contributes some combination of both, all are worthy of consideration from a power-building and mobilizing perspective.

These considerations accompany the broader socioeconomic power dynamics that transcend a particular community, such as race, class, gender, and sexual identity. Depending on your area, some of these factors may manifest as limitations on your formal power. Others may manifest as informal power: a group's willingness to let you meet with them based on your appearance, an individual's immediate dismissal of you when you say your name, a neighbor's openness toward you based on your children attending the same school as theirs, and so on. Race and gender, along with several other demographic signifiers, can dramatically impact the amount of informal power you retain when entering a room. Case in point: A white middle-aged man is more likely to hold informal power than a Black woman due to this country's history of segregation and institutionalized racism. As a result, your total power is heavily influenced by these (often unspoken) power dynamics, some explicitly tied to your rights and relationships in community-oriented work. In an ideal world, this would not be the case; unfortunately, we do not live in an ideal world, and for that reason we must be mindful of these dynamics as we work to empower ourselves, our allies, and our communities.

The forms of power are very rarely explicitly defined. Understanding a community and ultimately empowering individuals, however, requires understanding who holds and exercises formal and informal power in day-to-day affairs. While some may have formal titles, particularly those with formal power, the individuals with the most informal power likely will not. Finding these individuals, and figuring out how to comprehend the scope of their informal power, necessitates a study of place that we will further unpack in Part III.

Review Questions

- What formal power do you have now, have you had in the past, or do you want to have?
- What informal power do you have?

- What kind of power are you lacking? Who has it, and how could they work with you?
- How would you evaluate if you were gaining or losing formal or informal power?

NOTES

[1]Quoted in Roy Wilson, "Dr. King's Words About Nonviolence and Power," Martin Luther King Jr. Freedom Center, February 3, 2024, https://mlkfreedomcenter.org/dr-kings-words-about-nonviolence-power/.

3

Perspectives on Power

Now that we understand the forms of power, we need to understand how it functions and flows in our communities. Depending on who you ask, power—the ability to effect change—is either an authority that is heavily concentrated in certain hands and requires realignment or a force that is dormant and underutilized in a community. The perspective you adopt will inform the goals and motivations of your political activity.

The two schools of thought are not mutually exclusive. In fact, it is entirely possible for someone to hold both beliefs simultaneously. One way of doing so may occur when a person believes that too much power is concentrated in the wrong hands and only by mobilizing the people at large can power be realigned correctly. While this perspective is logically sound, it is important to understand the two perspectives independently. For simplicity purposes, we will refer to the first case, where power is concentrated in certain hands and requires reapportionment, as the **Realignment Perspective on Power** and to the second case, where power is inherently held by individuals and must be activated, as the **Awakening Perspective on Power**.

Realignment Perspective on Power

In the Realignment Perspective on Power, power is a limited resource. As such, that power is concentrated in certain hands, creating an imbalance, and thus requires realignment. The imbalance can involve a lack of rights, such as the rights of women to make decisions about their own bodies, or economic concerns, such as the various starting wages for workers at a company. In these and other cases of imbalance, power must be taken away from one party and given to another in order to better address the needs of impacted classes of people. For example, to improve their material conditions, power must be diverted from one class—the overwhelmingly male political class that makes decisions about women's bodily autonomy or the bosses who refuse to pay their workers more—to another—women or the workers. A corollary of this perspective is that those who are currently marginalized have insufficient power; otherwise, they would have the means of ending their marginalization without a redistribution of power. If workers had sufficient power to earn higher wages without confronting their bosses, they would use it to their benefit. Similarly, if women had the bodily autonomy to freely make decisions about their bodies, they would not need to enshrine such rights into law. As such, an organizing or advocacy campaign that addresses this imbalance seeks to move power from the hands of the powerful to the less powerful (or seemingly powerless). Success is measured by the power allotted to the formerly weaker party, now emboldened by the power they have gained. The passage of a law that grants a class of individuals a new right—one that disadvantages another class—is an example of success according to the Realignment Perspective.

The unequal distribution of limited power between different stakeholders necessitates the realignment effort. Similar to fixing an out-of-balance scale, shifting power from one stakeholder to another can result in equilibrium or a greater imbalance between the two. For a person or group to become more powerful, they must acquire power from somewhere or someone else. Because power is a limited resource, they cannot simply make themselves more powerful. If that were possible, power would not need to be redistributed between the two parties. Contrary to the alternative perspective, the Realignment Perspective on Power does not allow the less powerful party to pull themselves up by their bootstraps.

Awakening Perspective on Power

The Awakening Perspective on Power instead suggests that power is intrinsic to everyone; it is not a force that can be taken away. Additionally, power in this perspective is limitless. When the power within marginalized people has been suppressed, whether by socioeconomic, cultural, political, or personal factors, it must be uncovered and acted upon. The people must mobilize—awakening their power—to overcome the active power of those in control. Through this perspective, an organizing or advocacy campaign that addresses the imbalance does not redistribute power but rather leverages the power of one party against another. Success is therefore measured by the manner in which the formerly powerless are able to effect change in their material conditions—in other words, how they demonstrate their now awakened power. An individual who was previously afraid to speak publicly and deliver a testimony but who has since gained the oratory skill and confidence to amplify their voice at a public meeting is an example of a victory according to the Awakening Perspective.

In contrast to the Realignment Perspective, the Awakening Perspective suggests that power has no bounds; it can shrink, grow, or stagnate in an individual without immediate impacts on the power of others. Political education or broader participation in a campaign can result in an individual feeling like they have greater power over their present circumstances, particularly where they have developed new skills or overcome obstacles. The practice of these skills and act of overcoming obstacles that would have otherwise impeded an individual are indicators of awakened power. As a result, this perspective on power can be very personal in focus.

Comparing the Perspectives on Power

To better understand these perspectives on power, let's consider them side by side (see Table 1). As previously mentioned, the Realignment Perspective suggests that power is limited, whereas the Awakening Perspective views power as without bounds. Because the Realignment Perspective requires a shifting of power from one party to another, it is generally broader in focus than the Awakening Perspective, which focuses heavily on the power of an individual to effect change. Proponents of the Realignment Perspective measure success through the benefits achieved for the group that receives power. The Awakening Perspective, by contrast, identifies success on an individual level. Taken as a whole, the Realignment Perspective on Power seeks to address systemic inequities while the Awakening Perspective addresses an individual's feeling of powerlessness.

Table 1. Comparing Perspectives on Power

	Realignment	Awakening
Nature of Power	Limited	Boundless
Focus of Efforts	Systemic	Personal
Ultimate Beneficiary	Group	Individual
Inherent Problem	Inequity	Powerlessness
Application of Power	Static	Dynamic
Position in Time	Future	Present
Role in Power Change	A Sought-After End	A Means of Making Change

By comparing the two perspectives, we can identify other subtle differences. The Realignment Perspective sees power as an end in itself, the static objective that individuals or groups seek throughout their campaign. In the Awakening Perspective, power is a means of achieving change—a force to be leveraged in service of the campaign objective(s). Where the Realignment Perspective elevates power as the future prize for a successful campaign, the Awakening Perspective positions power as a tool used in the present to succeed in that campaign.

From here, we can see clearly that these perspectives are significantly divergent on the nature and application of power. Advocates of social justice may be encouraged by the Realignment Perspective's systemic worldview and explicit focus on inequity as a problem that needs solving. The Awakening Perspective, while decidedly more individualistic, takes a more active approach to using power to achieve change. Because both perspectives are valid, choosing one over the other ignores the reality that each is necessary for enacting social change.

At their core, political movements constitute the mobilization of individuals to fight for a larger cause. In other words, political movements center on individuals combining and leveraging their cooperative *awakening* to *realign* power from one group to another. No systemic change would be possible without people being somewhat confident in their own power to effect that change. Likewise, no individual empowerment is possible without an understanding of the systemic shifts that have preceded our present moment. We all stand on the shoulders of giants, and the ubiquity of that cliché only reinforces the urgency of our collective efforts.

How Perspectives on Power Inform Community-Building Work

Power is not simply an application of realignment or awakening; it is both. A pure proponent of the Realignment Perspective considers power like a coin that passes hands over the course of history. A pure proponent of the Awakening Perspective considers power like a seed that can be nurtured or neglected. As an individual who engages with people who support either or both, the best thing you can do is develop an understanding of both sides while expanding your neighbors', colleagues', and allies' perspectives on power.

Before any engagement with public-facing work, you must interrogate your own inherent perspective on power. Do you find yourself drawn to the Realignment or Awakening Perspective on Power? As indicated in the previous section, neither approach is entirely wrong; each is only half-right. Both perspectives are necessary to enact social change on a sustainable scale. If you want to succeed in your own local endeavors, an appreciation of both sides is necessary. At worst, you will have lengthy discussions on the nature and application of power. At best, you will uplift supporters of both perspectives and allow them to blend into your spaces to achieve the kind of sustainable social movements that can be protected and built upon for years to come.

To fulfill such lofty ambitions, you must tailor your own actions to both perspectives on power. You cannot simply rely on those with a Realignment Perspective to inspire others and build movements for change: A campaign to win tangible policy shifts cannot happen without people tapping into their own power. Similarly, reclaiming that power does not always translate into systemic shifts of rights and protections: The feeling of a powerful protest alone is insufficient to secure a policy victory for the protesters. A synergy of the two perspectives is necessary. As such, both must be welcome and supported in the spaces you facilitate, rally, and lead.

For example, the Realignment Perspective lends itself well to the overall structure of an organizing and advocacy campaign: Shifting power from one party to another provides a direct way to organize and build solidarity among the people you plan to engage. The achievement of a policy or program that redistributes power between parties is a clear endpoint, and the enactment of said policy is ideally tangible and compelling enough to keep participants engaged.

Yet, to achieve this shift, you may need to adopt the Awakening Perspective. At the very least, a potential policy initiative must have some demonstrable level of support in order to even be considered. Whether measured by physical presence in public meetings, phone calls to legislative officials, or the number of speakers at a rally, that support is often best accomplished by those who are convinced of their own power: their capacity to make a difference by sitting in on public meetings, calling elected officials, or speaking at a rally. These actions also provide opportunities for those feeling powerless to reassert their power. The actions therefore serve as a means of demonstrating awakened power and building the pressure necessary to ultimately realign power. With enough individuals awakening their own power over the course of a campaign, the objectives defined through the Realignment Perspective become possible.

It is also valuable to consider how the decision-makers you are engaging perceive power. Those who come from a purely Realignment Perspective will see power as a limited resource and, as such, may be intimidated by efforts to redistribute power from those who have it, such as themselves. By contrast, decision-makers on the side of the Awakening Perspective may be easier to engage as their own power is not necessarily threatened by the actions of you or your allies. While the latter sounds preferable, the reality is that, as with participants in an organizing or advocacy effort, decision-makers need to take both perspectives. An elected official who applauds a person giving public testimony but does not understand the importance of tangibly reallocating power is potentially as problematic as an elected official who refuses to relinquish any of their power or to redistribute power from other stakeholders.

An Endangered Understanding of Power

While the perspectives and forms of power establish a methodology for understanding power, the present political moment is particularly dangerous because of the damage being done to the institutions that sustain many of these basic concepts. Formal power depends on the strength of the institutions that originally defined it. Rights are one of the most easily understood representations of formal power. However, if the institutions behind these rights are continually undermined or ignored, those institutions—laws—become less respected and, therefore, weaker. As a result, the rights afforded by laws may become harder to enforce, causing a downward spiral: Weakening the institutions (laws) that define rights weakens those rights. The weakened rights result in weaker institutions (laws), which again weaken rights, and the cycle repeats. Eventually, rights will become so weak as to be irrelevant. The diminishing of the institutions that define formal power, including but not limited to rights, is a fundamental threat to the social, political, and economic order that every person currently inhabits.

Additionally, formal power is the most likely type to be redistributed in the Realignment Perspective. Rights again provide an illustrative example: When institutions grant rights to individuals, those rights are codified by law and enforced through those institutions. The rights belong not to a specific individual, but to a class of individuals (women, children, immigrants, etc.). The universality of rights is part of their appeal; every individual within a class does not need to directly advocate for those rights to receive them. Merely being in the given class grants that formal power.

Continually diminishing the institutions of formal power greatly reduces the appeal of working to redistribute that power. One may prefer to simply build relationships with the right individuals (informal power) instead of seeking to establish a right or protection for a whole class of people. While developing informal power is valuable for building community, it should not be an individual's only source of power. A child should not be expected to advocate for their own rights; a victim of abuse should have automatic protections to address the injustices they have suffered. Contemporary society has been built on a foundation of certain inalienable rights, which by their very nature are not contingent upon who knows whom. The rights of citizens, residents, children, and other vulnerable individuals should not be subject to personal relationships; formal power provides an umbrella for all of these individuals as general categories.

Undermining formal power and delegitimizing the Realignment Perspective on Power could have devastating impacts for every individual who enjoys that formal power and the mechanisms that enabled it—which is to say every person living in the United States of America. The weakening of formal power may shift the focus to informal power, but a society dictated entirely by relationships and without recognition of rights or generalized credentials is hardly a society at all. What is the value in advocating for a new law if the institutions that enforce that law are weak? What are governmental checks and balances to a group that rejects their legally defined responsibilities? What are constitutional rights in a society that ignores the Constitution? Representative government as a concept is built on the legitimacy of formal power and on the allotment of power made through the Realignment Perspective. The dismantling of these concepts therefore dismantles the concept of representative government itself. While philosophers have theorized about the state of nature as a period before civil society,[1] the current American moment is dangerous as it puts us on a path where a state of nature is in our potential future, not our past.

The search for equilibrium between formal and informal power is the foundation upon which civil society can generally function. Although no society has managed to perfect this balancing act, the solution to injustice is better leveraging apportioned rights—through the Realignment Perspective—and mobilized relationships—through the Awakening Perspective—to preserve and expand those protections for the generations to come. By contrast, dismantling these concepts rejects the contemporary history of power and threatens the livelihood of every person reliant on their rights to function. Understanding this ideological threat and the importance of directly confronting it is necessary for appreciating the urgency of organizing and advocacy work in this moment.

Review Questions

- Are there certain types of people who tend to ascribe to a certain perspective on power? For example, do teachers, law enforcement, local elected officials, and wealthy or poor neighbors have a similar perspective on power? How would you engage with them?
- Given that the terms *Realignment Perspective* and *Awakening Perspective* are not commonly used, how would you go about figuring out a person's perspective on power?
- Which perspective on power appeals more to your understanding of politics? Have you experienced a realignment or awakening of power?
- How would you balance the need for both perspectives of power in your organizing and advocacy campaigns?

NOTES

[1] Thomas Hobbes, *Leviathan* (1651; Project Gutenberg, eds. Edward White and David Widger, 2025), https://www.gutenberg.org/cache/epub/3207/pg3207-images.html.

APPLIED SKILLS

The philosophers have only interpreted the world, in various ways. The point, however, is to change it.

—KARL MARX

Developing your own political theory is an enormous task. Acting on that ideology, sharing it with others, and mobilizing with them to make your community a better place is another task entirely. And while a great deal of the work of political theory can be accomplished alone, the application of that theory requires the engagement of other people. In its simplest form, that engagement is dialogue. However, organizers and advocates do not merely talk to others; they engage them, lead them, and challenge them to deepen their own understanding as they take action. In the best cases, organizers and advocates develop people as leaders as well.

Consider our definition of power, introduced in Chapter 1. "The ability to achieve purpose"[1] means nothing without action. In other words, having power and using power are entirely different matters. Where Part I sought to develop an understanding of power, Part II seeks to encourage action through practical skill development. Having the ability to do good is not the same as doing good. Applying that ability through intentional and strategic actions is what differentiates those who use power, those who hoard their power, and those who have no power at all.

Developing and refining the skills necessary to enact change—to achieve purpose—is the ongoing work of an organizer and advocate. And while many skills are worth developing given the circumstances, the following chapters will focus on three generally valuable skills in organizing, advocacy, and community-building spaces. Facilitation allows you to engage with your allies effectively. Public speaking hones your ability to communicate with the wider world. Power mapping equips you and your allies with the ability to visualize campaign strategy and reflect upon its efficacy. Like a muscle gaining strength through exercise, the more you use these skills, the more effective and successful your efforts will be.

NOTES

[1] Quoted in Roy Wilson, "Dr. King's Words About Nonviolence and Power," Martin Luther King Jr. Freedom Center, February 3, 2024, https://mlkfreedomcenter.org/dr-kings-words-about-nonviolence-power/.

4

Meeting Facilitation

Facilitation is simply a matter of making things easier. It is not inherently tied to meetings. When considering the role of organizers and advocates, recognize them as facilitators of change. In other words, they make achieving change easier. That change can be the establishment of new policy or the mobilization of people to take bold public action. However, before organizers or advocates can achieve these more public and visual changes, they will need to practice the ability to achieve change on a smaller scale, such as through a meeting of like-minded individuals.

While considerably less visible than a rally or public action, successful meeting facilitation can just as decisively change the direction of a campaign. While organizers and advocates may be popularized as figures on the vanguard of a demonstration, their skill in running a meeting is less glamorous but more grounded and arguably more impactful. As a facilitator, your role is not to fill silences, but to make it easier for others to fill those silences. Nor is your role to be the expert in the room, but to make it easier for the expertise of others to emerge. During a meeting, your voice as a facilitator is likely the least important in the room. However, after a meeting, your *role* may be remembered as the most important.

As a facilitator, what you say is less important than what you do to enable others to participate—how you enable them to change the awkward silence in a room into strategic, intentional, and collaborative dialogue. If you are skillful enough, your actions will go largely unnoticed as the conversation naturally flows from one person to another, from problem to solution, solution to action, or impassioned plea to resolved commitment. By the end of a meeting, the mark of a good facilitator is that almost every person can conclude "this was not a waste of my time." Better is certainly possible, but to expect every meeting to be a life-changing experience for every participant is a bit of a high bar, even for the best facilitators. Small changes facilitate big changes, and a skilled facilitator ensures those changes happen. In this way, you may not be remembered for what you said or what you did, but your handling of a meeting, and how it made people feel, is what will bring participants into your broader campaign efforts.

What a Facilitator Is (And Is Not)

A facilitator is not the expert in the room. Generally, if a meeting is going to involve some discussion on a topic, you do not want your facilitator to have the most expertise in the topic area. Why? Because it is not a facilitator's job to be an active participant in a group discussion. The facilitator asks questions, but they often do not provide their own answers. Doing so could make the facilitator seem biased and possibly undermine their credibility with meeting participants. Consider a facilitator as a meeting midwife. A midwife's role is not to create life, but to support parents as they prepare to bring life into the world. Similarly, facilitators lead meetings not to give answers, but to support the group as they prepare to find the answer for themselves.

Granted, a facilitator should have some level of understanding of what will be discussed, but that understanding can absolutely be matched and superseded by others in the meeting space. Additionally, if a person has particularly strong feelings about the meeting topic, they will not likely be a good facilitator, simply because the (generally neutral) facilitator role restricts the expression of those strong feelings. If someone wants to express their opinions in a meeting, they should be empowered to do so as a participant. A facilitator must be perceived as neutral because participants may not otherwise feel comfortable enough to join the discussion. No one will want to participate if they feel their perspective is unwelcome or likely to be judged by the group. The facilitator, in this regard, sets the tone of acceptance for the entire group. Particularly in spaces where groups must make difficult decisions, a facilitator's goal should be to achieve their group's trust and respect. Admittedly, this is a difficult balance, as "neutrality" is based upon the participants in the room. As we will soon discuss, meeting participants are not a random assortment of individuals from the general public, but rather a self-selected group of individuals who ascribe to a meeting's purpose and outcome. As such, the facilitator is "neutral" inasmuch as one can be neutral after an explicitly stated purpose and outcome for a meeting is shared with the wider public.

When a facilitator makes participants comfortable enough to express their opinions in a meeting, that facilitator does not decide who is right or wrong. Rather, they encourage the group to determine a process for collective decision-making. Sometimes, group agreement cannot be reached, and that is fine. A facilitator generally does not force a group to make decisions it is unprepared to make. The role of a facilitator, in the context of meetings for social justice, is to help a group achieve their stated objectives.

Purpose, Outcome, and Process

Whether explicitly stated or implied, any meeting worth attending includes some critical elements: an understanding of why the meeting is being held, a goal for the meeting participants to reach by the end of the meeting, and a plan for putting the relevant pieces in place in order for them to achieve that goal. These three elements make up a meeting's purpose, outcome, and process, also known as a POP.

Purpose serves to prevent a meeting's ultimate condemnation: "Why did we hold that meeting?" While people may attend a meeting for various purposes (socializing with like-minded individuals, grandstanding, troubleshooting a pressing issue, etc.), a stated purpose creates a shared goal for everyone in the room. For example, a meeting could be held for participants to process recent local events and to brainstorm immediate actions in response. An explicitly shared purpose also creates an initial layer of group accountability. Sharing the purpose of a meeting before and at the beginning of a meeting not only ensures a shared expectation of what will be discussed and what will be left out; it also allows people to self-select to attend or skip the meeting. This makes it easier for a facilitator to steer group discussions away from tangents or rabbit holes and back to the purpose. As we'll soon explore, this initial layer of accountability will be increasingly necessary in meeting facilitation.

While a meeting's purpose brings everyone together, its *outcome* is the point that everyone will (hopefully) reach by the end of the meeting. To build upon the earlier example of people coming together to process local events and brainstorm immediate actions, the outcome could be participants leaving with new group relationships, exchanging phone numbers and emails, and making plans to meet in smaller groups to coordinate future activities. Again, sharing the outcome with participants ahead of time is valuable, as it gives everyone a realistic expectation of where the facilitator expects the meeting to conclude. While we can easily see the strong connection between purpose and outcome, they are not the same. A meeting's purpose is what brings people in; a meeting's outcome is what they leave with. For a facilitator, a clear outcome is vital to keeping the group focused and action-oriented. Tangents will be introduced, and verbosity will inevitably occur, but planning for an explicit outcome gives everyone a clear understanding of where they are expected to end up by the end of their time together.

With these pieces in place, a meeting's *process* is the series of activities or actions that ensure all participants begin at the same starting point (purpose) and reach the same ending point (outcome). While a meeting's agenda plays an enormous part, the meeting's process includes the formation of the agenda and every component tied to its implementation. Where will the meeting take place—online, in-person, or a hybrid of the two? How will the meeting be set up to accommodate everyone, regardless of how they attend? When should people arrive to help with setup, and how many volunteers will be needed? How will the agenda and meeting information be shared with participants ahead of and during the meeting? Each of these questions can spin off into several others, all of which should be considered, if not completely answered, by the meeting's facilitator. (Refer to the appendix for an event planning checklist.) Granted, many of these questions will become easier to answer after a few meetings, but failing to consider them ahead of time can be tremendously risky. Time spent setting up extra tables for food or troubleshooting the projector is time spent distracting participants from focusing on the meeting's purpose or working toward its outcome. Your goal as the facilitator is to make discussions flow easily, and improperly examining and executing the meeting's process interrupts that flow, undermining the preparations you may have made elsewhere.

Agendas

A meeting's agenda is not a to-do list, though thinking of it as such can be incredibly tempting. The agenda should clarify the activities and actions expected of attendees. Ideally, it should indicate how participants will engage with these activities and actions (e.g., "Community Processing," "Group Discussion," and "Close-Out"). If the group plans to tackle particularly important questions, they should be written in the agenda. Agendas more closely resemble road maps than to-do lists in that a person should be able to join a meeting at any point and generally understand what has been covered, what's currently going on, and where the discussion will conclude by the meeting's end.

Figure 2. Sample Meeting Agenda

Purpose: *Build community as we process recent local events and brainstorm ways to collectively respond.*

Outcome: *Participants will leave with new relationships and small groups formed to carry brainstormed ideas forward.*

Process: *The meeting will be held in-person at ABC Community Center (space acquired and donated by Commissioner Jones) from 5 to 7 p.m., with food being purchased by Dr. Ortiz and childcare being offered by Care Collective. Volunteers will arrive at 4:15 to set up space, test out the audiovisual equipment, prop the door open, ensure accessibility according to the Americans with Disabilities Act, meet the food delivery person at 4:30, and prep the sign-in table.*

- **Welcome and Level Setting** (10 minutes)
  - Facilitator: T. Alker
  - Logistics: Childcare, restrooms, and Wi-Fi
  - Introduction: Give your name, how you heard about this meeting, and one word to describe your emotions in this moment
- **Reviewing Current Local Events** (10 minutes)
  - Speaker: Commissioner Jones
  - PowerPoint presentation
- **Community Processing** (30 minutes)
  - In breakout groups of four or five, answer the following:
    - What resonated most from the presentation?
    - What should the community do in response?
  - Have one speaker ready to share your answers with the larger group
  - Be sure to reintroduce yourselves!
- **Group Discussion** (30 minutes)
  - Breakout Group Report-Outs
  - Questions for Discussion
    - What are the commonalities between the groups? What are the differences?
    - What should the community do in response? (List the top four responses on the projector screen.)
    - Which actions are most compelling? (Stand-Up/Sit-Down Activity)
      - Why is this action most compelling to you?
      - What can you personally do to move this action forward?
- **Close-Out** (10 minutes)
  - Reintroductions to your neighbor
    - Name
    - How you are feeling right now
    - Way to stay in touch before the next meeting
  - Reminders
    - Sign-in sheet
    - Social media handles

As such, certain elements found in many meeting agendas provide a good foundation for a facilitator. A meeting's *welcome* can be as informal as tapping a microphone and saying hi to everyone or as formal as gaveling in and calling the meeting to order. Often, the welcome includes the name of the meeting, the meeting's purpose and outcome, and any logistical notes, such as restrooms and refreshments. Particularly in the case of participatory meetings, considerable time should be set aside for *meeting activities* that allow attendees to engage with one another, whether in small breakout groups, stand-up/sit-down activities, or games. (A sample meeting activity is provided in the appendix.) How to facilitate this engagement largely depends on the meeting's purpose, its outcome, and the participating attendees. Finally, the facilitator should end the meeting with some form of *close-out* and *next steps.* You can spend this time assessing if the meeting achieved its purpose and outcome, and providing actionable steps for the attendees. The sample agenda in Figure 2, also available in the appendix, corresponds to the POP described in the previous sections.

Obviously, several elements in this agenda (meals, breaks, etc.) could be changed, but it is useful to illustrate here that the purpose, outcome, and process help to guide the meeting agenda. Because community building is a stated goal in the purpose, activities that create opportunities to build relationships are vital to include throughout the meeting. Similarly, if the meeting were hybrid, the facilitator would need to make several changes to the agenda to ensure everyone is engaged (would virtual participants, for example, form their own breakout group?). If the meeting's purpose or outcome changed, the agenda—a component of the meeting's process—would likely need to shift as well.

Community Agreements

An important element of any meeting is a strong set of community agreements. In cases where everyone knows each other, the meeting's community agreements may go largely unspoken. However, in meetings where not all participants know each other, setting a shared standard for engagement is crucial. The following are some of the basic questions community agreements should answer:

- Do participants need to raise their hand to speak?
- Can participants or presenters record or take pictures during this meeting?
- How will the facilitator and full group handle the situation if someone says something offensive?
- How will the facilitator and full group address it if someone starts monologuing or speechifying?

Community agreements can get very specific. At the very least, they set the ground rules for how everyone participates in a meeting. Perhaps most importantly, community agreements belong to the community. In other words, they should be enforced not simply by the facilitator, but by everyone in the meeting. This shared sense of accountability creates shared ownership of meeting spaces and the topics under discussion. As a result, people become more invested, whether in their passion for a topic or in their commitment to seeing everyone participate equitably in a meeting space.

Facilitation as Art, Not Science

Sometimes, the agenda needs to change, the POP proves overly ambitious, or a tangent turns out to be far more pressing than the original plan. Meeting facilitation is more art than science: It involves no immutable facts or transcendent laws. Even the beloved *Robert's Rules of Order*[1] are subject to the broader reality of meetings: people. Perhaps an individual experienced a traumatic event immediately before the meeting; perhaps a major positive development makes your initially planned agenda unnecessary; perhaps your group is further along in an issue than you thought. These and many other factors are valid reasons to scrap your agenda and go in another direction.

As you gain experience facilitating, you will develop a better sense of whether or not your POP and agenda resonate with the group. This skill develops as you begin to understand that a meeting's POP and agenda form a semi-explicit agreement between you as the facilitator and those attending the meeting. Participants may want to say or do various different things in a meeting, but they all generally expect the purpose, outcome, and process to happen as explained. They similarly expect the agenda to be followed to achieve the POP. The participants have agreed to go on a ride, both by attending and by engaging in meeting activities; the facilitator has agreed to help them reach their destination.

Whether a meeting is proceeding well or poorly, checking in on your group's feelings is generally good practice. Are the attendees excited or despondent? Irritated or appreciated? Especially in those moments of blank stares and awkward silence, stepping back and asking the broader question, "Is everyone feeling OK? Is this resonating with folks, or do we need a break?" can be worth a try. Similarly, when participants are eagerly in discussion on a particular topic but the agenda indicates it is time to move on, a perceptive facilitator creates an opportunity for the group to continue their discussion or stick to the agenda. In either silent or vibrant meetings, a facilitator responds to the energy of meeting participants.

Creating a POP, an agenda, and community agreements should always be a collaborative process between a facilitator and participants. While there is often only one facilitator, the group as a whole should have some input on the meeting structure and objectives. Similarly, discarding the POP and/or agenda should be a collaborative decision. Shifting gears completely can be difficult; it should come as no surprise, then, that the facilitator's role, as always, is to make this seem easy.

Review Questions

- What do you think would make you a good facilitator? What would make facilitation challenging?

- Have you attended a recent meeting that had a clear purpose and outcome? What do you think was the process for that meeting?
- What kinds of activities might your meeting attendees enjoy? How can you make your meetings more memorable?
- Have you ever participated in a meeting where the agenda was radically changed partway through the meeting? How did you react to that change?

NOTES

[1]General Henry M. Robert, Sarah Corbin Robert, Henry M. Robert III, William J. Evans, Daniel H. Honemann, Thomas J. Balch, Daniel E. Seabold, and Shmuel Gerber, *Robert's Rules of Order*, 12th ed. (PublicAffairs, 2020).

5

Public Speaking

In a time of so much polarization and heated rhetoric, speaking publicly on any matter, let alone the issues that matter most to you personally, can be very intimidating. Even in less turbulent times, public speaking can be a source of great anxiety. Yet few skills are as central to a functional democracy as the ability to speak up. Whether on stage at a group meeting, at a podium during a public hearing, or in front of cameras at an event, public speaking can inspire your allies, shift local opinions, and demonstrate power in an otherwise chaotic time.

For the purposes of this chapter, we will focus on public speaking that makes an argument and calls for action. In such circumstances, the speaker is both the messenger of the argument and the one calling for action. These roles are related but distinct, specifically because the resonance of the argument and the resonance of the call to action depend on different factors:

- A speech's argument relies upon a clear framing of the problem, solution, and action.
- A speech's call to action relies upon the argument *and* the speaker making a connection with their audience.

Effective public speakers can articulate a problem, solution, and action while making effective connections with their audience. Understanding that public speaking requires this balanced approach, you should consider the following questions in preparation.

Why Are You Talking?

Understanding *why* you want to speak is just as important, if not more so, than *what* you want to say. To borrow from the previous chapter, understanding your why is to define the purpose of your speech. Some people feel compelled to make themselves heard on a personal or urgent issue. Others may want to speak on behalf of others who are unable to advocate for themselves. Others still might just need the catharsis. None of these motivations are inherently good or bad, but understanding which of these reasons or others compels you to speak can help put you in the right frame of mind to speak publicly. If your why is rooted in personal and emotional experience, you are not likely to first turn to statistical data to make your point. By contrast, if your why is rooted in addressing a falsehood, presenting counterevidence to the claim may seem more important than highlighting how the falsehood affects you personally. This is not to suggest that emotionally motivated speakers should avoid facts and figures, or that content experts should avoid appeals to emotion. Rather, it is important to understand why you wish to speak so that you can deliver your message in such a way that it most strongly appeals to your intended audience, whether it's your base, your opposition, or the undecided folks in the middle. Particularly in the context of organizing and advocacy, one reason why you may wish to talk is to convince people to take action on an issue. In this case, your why is to convey an argument—one that you hope will compel people to act.

Who Is Your Audience?

After understanding why you want to speak publicly, your intended audience is worth considering. This may not always be obvious. Speaking at an event may be about reaching the general public who will read about the event later. Addressing a government body during the public comment period could be about reaching the elected officials or getting a notable quote in the press. Your intended audience could be sitting opposite or alongside you. Your words may be intended to win over the general public, challenge entrenched power, or rally your allies to wield their own power.

After identifying your primary audience, you can tailor your remarks to that audience: What would be compelling to them? What would hold their attention? If you are speaking with a clear call to action in mind, what sort of comments would compel your audience to act? At the same time, what kinds of framing or information would alienate them? Tailoring your remarks can make the difference between success and failure in your efforts.

When speaking to key decision-makers, you must also understand what kind of comments will move them in the direction you want. Clearly, no politician likes getting yelled at by a constituent, but understanding what information a politician does like is important. Are they moved by quantitative data, constituents' lived experiences, or demonstrable knowledge of relevant policy? You may find it cathartic to demean and insult decision-makers on the cusp of making a bad decision, but it is strategically better to focus on convincing them in the moments before a crucial vote. Politicians are, after all, human, and as such, you can often find ways to get through to them that do not require a suitcase full of money. This can also apply in the other direction, where a politician will vote against their best interest simply because of how someone made them feel. This is not to suggest politicians deserve continuous adulation, but understanding when and how to most effectively criticize them, particularly when speaking during public meetings or hearings, is a vital tool for both winning them over and achieving your desired political outcome.

In the case of an audience primarily comprising your allies, it is similarly important to understand what motivates them. As with key decision-makers, some in your coalition will be motivated by hard numbers and statistics, others by their lived experience, and others by their interest in advancing a cause. Speaking to all of these is a delicate balance, but it serves the dual purpose of framing your cause. A person speaking on an issue who focuses entirely on statistics may be construed as elitist, while a speaker focusing on direct experience may be ignored based on lack of hard data. Delivering remarks that both rally your allies and anticipate criticism is a skill set that takes experience to develop, but practice makes it possible.

What Will They Remember?

As with facilitation in Chapter 4, an element of successful public speaking is people's feelings. What you want people to remember from your remarks is analogous to a meeting's outcome, where you want people to end. How your public speaking makes people feel can be split into two categories: how people remember you and how people remember what you said. A public speaker who jumps at the opportunity to provide their opinion in any pregnant pause is likely to make a very different impression than a public speaker who deliberately chooses when to speak and when to stay silent. How you speak will greatly influence how you are remembered, by not only your intended audience but anyone else who hears you. Similarly, depending on how often you plan to speak publicly, you may develop a reputation as a public speaker on given topics—a distinction you can leverage or subvert to your benefit, assuming you accept the notoriety you receive.

How people remember you may be less important than how they remember what you said. While several factors beyond your control can influence how people remember you, ensuring the audience retains the right takeaways from your public comments falls more squarely within your control. Repetition is an obvious way to get your audience to remember key points—whether they are data points, emotional appeals, or frames of understanding a situation. How you deliver your remarks, whether through vivid imagery or cold hard logic, can resonate with different audiences. Regardless of your method, a generally good practice is to have key takeaways or themes for public remarks. Presenting too many points, statistics, or anecdotes can overwhelm your audience, leading to nothing sticking or, worse yet, running out of time. By contrast, there is no such thing as having too few points, assuming you present at least one. Even a single key point can be emphasized and reiterated in different ways.

Who Are You?

At its core, public speaking means conveying yourself to the world. Whether that projection is accurate is up to you. How you convey yourself in public may mirror your true personal identity. Others may wear their public speaking persona like a mask. In either case, how you speak publicly is ultimately up to you. You can draw inspiration from others, but whether you present a mask or your true self, you should always speak in a way that is all your own. For example, two people can read the exact same speech but deliver it in entirely different ways. Their body language, eye contact, gesturing, tone of voice, and reading pace can result in different deliveries. Additionally, the why and audience for each speaker may differ dramatically. All of these factors converge to create a completely different public speaking experience. Each is unique to the individual. They may want to vary their approach as they gain comfortability with their speech, but the overall public speaking experience will still be all their own. All of this serves to say that each public speaker will be different in their style and approach, and while some public speaking traits are generally looked upon more favorably (eye contact, an even speaking pace, etc.), the most important factor behind public speaking is the speaker themselves. Do not lose yourself in what you want to say. Even if you need to wear a mask, decorate that mask to make sure it is entirely your own.

Where Will You Speak?

When preparing to speak publicly, one of your biggest considerations should be the venue of your remarks. Where you speak largely influences several of the aforementioned questions, and it also informs other factors such as your time limit, use of visual aids, and opportunity to take questions. Some spaces, such as public meetings, may have strict rules on when individuals may speak, for how long, and on what specific topic. Understanding the basic parameters of these spaces is crucial to remaining calm and ensuring your comments resonate enough to achieve their desired impact. Consider the following two venues for public speaking:

- *Public Hearing:* A formal meeting of a local, county, state, or federal entity to debate whether to enact or reject a given piece of legislation. The speakers are limited to a set duration of time, such as five minutes; may not use any visual aids; may only directly address the governmental officials presiding over the meeting; and must limit their remarks to the legislation under consideration. In some circumstances, speakers are required to sign up before speaking. Speakers may be asked questions by members of the voting body, ranging in perspective from openly hostile to genuinely supportive, but not necessarily. Participation from the audience, such as applause or boos, will only shorten the speaker's limited time and is generally frowned upon.
- *News Conference:* A gathering of like-minded individuals to call attention to a particular issue in front of the press. Speakers are strategically identified ahead of time to address different aspects of the selected issue. While they may not have a formal

time limit, each speaker must be mindful of time as members of the press may not stay for the full event. Visual aids are often well received, such as bags of trash to demonstrate the impact of a community park cleanup. Speakers have some flexibility to weave in related topics, again subject to the overall strategy of the event. Press outlets may come with questions, and reporters will appreciate concise and resonant responses, often repeating them as quotes in follow-up coverage. Participation from the audience, such as applause or boos, may help to amplify the speaker's message and inform the narrative that the press will convey in follow-up coverage.

Learning as much as possible about your venue before you speak helps to ensure you present your remarks confidently and effectively. The physical space is also important, both in considering your audience and in calming anxieties. For example, placement and type of microphone may be the kind of unexpected shift that can throw off an inexperienced public speaker. In the case of public hearings and news conferences, it's useful to know if your audience supports you, opposes you, or is generally neutral. This can help you anticipate supportive or detractive reactions from the crowd. It also can help you maintain your cool in the moment. Unfortunately, and typically in the case of public debates, the first person to lose their cool is often remembered poorly. While you cannot control what others say or do, you can control your reaction (or lack thereof). In cases that involve a strict time limit in a public hearing, it may be preferable to have a script. Particularly if you plan to cite statistics, bringing extra copies of your remarks so elected officials can follow along with your comments is helpful. If not, or if you feel particularly confident, perhaps a list of key talking points is sufficient. Practicing remarks in front of a mirror may feel awkward, but getting used to seeing eyes staring back at you while you speak can help ease nervousness when the real thing happens. As with all skills, this gets easier with practice. (For a public speaking checklist, refer to the appendix.)

How Will You Engage With the Press?

While much of the previous guidance still applies in the case of talking to the press, some particular nuances are worth unpacking when a reporter approaches you at an event or contacts you over the phone. For one, everything you say to the reporter is on the record, meaning that it can be directly attributed to you, unless otherwise indicated. This is important specifically because while a one-on-one conversation with a reporter is not exactly public speaking in the way a news conference is, the result is effectively the same: Your words will be used to inform a story. To this end, some reporters will record your comments when you speak with them—essentially the equivalent of speaking into a microphone at a news conference. While speaking one-on-one with a reporter may feel more personal and comfortable, maintaining the same level of message discipline and consistency as when speaking in front of a crowd is crucial.

At the same time, because the conversation is one-on-one, you can get a better understanding of the reporter's interests by asking them questions as well. Knowing what they plan to write about, or how they plan to frame the story, can give you insights that will inform your comments. A business reporter who covers real estate news is less likely to be interested in the human impacts of a new megadevelopment, but they may be very interested in job numbers and other economic impacts. A one-on-one conversation provides the opportunity for you to discover this information in ways a press conference could not. Developing comfortability speaking one-on-one with the press creates other opportunities as well, including being a point of contact or source for future stories and developing a direct line for media to cover future relevant events.

Review Questions

- Who is a compelling public speaker? What about them is compelling?
- What, if anything, intimidates you about public speaking? How can you prepare yourself to address that concern?
- Where do you see yourself doing public speaking? Are there other venues you might speak in?
- How do you prepare yourself to speak publicly?

6

Power Mapping

Power maps are living documents, providing a snapshot of the relevant stakeholders and their relationships with regard to a particular issue, in this chapter referred to as a *position* or *agenda*. Because they focus so much on relationships between individuals and groups, power maps constantly need updating. Individuals and groups can become more or less aligned with your position or agenda, and their power can similarly rise and fall. As the decline of one stakeholder often corresponds with the rise of another, the Realignment Perspective on Power is easy to visualize using a power map. The Awakening Perspective on Power can similarly be visualized through an individual or group's independent power growth, stagnation, or decline over the course of a campaign. At their core, power maps should provide some guidance for determining your key targets, potential allies, and likely opposition, allowing you to leverage this vital information to develop your strategy for advancing an issue or cause.

The Basics of Power Mapping

Power maps can take many different forms. The "best" version of a power map is the one that works best for you and the people you aim to organize. While I have used the following type of power map[1] over the years, you can utilize the template provided in Figure 3, enlarged in the appendix for ease of use, in many different ways.

Our Agenda		Opposing Agenda
10. Decisive in Decision-Making		10. Decisive in Decision-Making
8. Active in Decision-Making		8. Active in Decision-Making
6. Major Influence in Decision-Making		6. Major Influence in Decision-Making
4. Taken into Account		4. Taken into Account
2. Can Get Attention		2. Can Get Attention
0. Not on Radar		0. Not on Radar

Die Hard — Active Support — Inclined to Support — Neutral — Inclined to Support — Active Support — Die Hard

Figure 3. Blank Power Map

The x-axis (alignment axis) illustrates alignment with your agenda, with points farthest to the left being most aligned and points farthest to the right being most opposed. The middle indicates neutrality or indecision. The y-axis (power axis) illustrates the power to enact your agenda, with the bottommost points being largely inconsequential and the topmost points being decisive. Taken together, these points can help you calibrate strategy with allies or anticipate challenges from opposition. (See Figure 4 for an explanation of the levels of power.)

Prior to attempting to arrange stakeholders on a power map, defining your agenda is critical. What issue or cause do you wish to illustrate on your power map? The more specificity you can provide, the better. For example, mapping individuals and groups according to their perspective on a specific piece of legislation is easier than mapping their views toward a broader cause like "walkability." This is because broad topics often lack the nuances necessary to understand an individual or group's exact placement on a power map. For example, an official might generally support crosswalks but oppose directing transit funding toward pedestrian infrastructure in the upcoming city budget, preferring instead to apply for federal funds. If you attempt to plot multiple points under such a broad agenda, your map may not be very accurate or informative. The more specific you can make your agenda, the more precisely you will be able to place stakeholders on your power map. In the case of walkability, a more specific agenda could be to "increase municipal funding for community crosswalks in the upcoming city budget."

With a clear and specific agenda defined, you can begin to plot stakeholders on your map. A good place to start is by mapping *yourself*, either as an individual or as an organization. Because you are likely to be mapping your own agenda, your placement on the alignment axis will clearly fall into the "Die-Hard" category. As a visual representation of your current power to enact the agenda you defined, however, your placement on the power axis can be difficult to determine. In the case of legislative campaigns, you are likely not among the top rungs of power, typically populated by the elected officials who hold voting, signing, or veto power—formal power—on your issue. Falling on the lower end of the power axis is nothing to be ashamed of, especially as it provides an opportunity for you to see your individual or group's power increase over the course of a campaign.

With an understanding of your own placement on the power map, the next most logical placements would center on the groups or individuals who have the formal power to give you what you want—in other words, the *decision-makers*. In a legislative campaign, this would include the bill sponsor, co-sponsors, and other elected officials involved in the passage of legislation you support or oppose.

While the exact ranking can be somewhat subjective, consider the following framework when considering each level of power on the y-axis of the power map:

0. Not on Radar: Generally the category where any unengaged person on the street would fall.

2. Can Get Attention: Individuals or organizations who could effectively garner the attention of decision-makers.

4. Taken Into Account: Individuals or organizations who could write a letter or make a phone call to a decision-maker and get a genuine response.

6. Major Influence in Decision-Making: Individuals or organizations who can get a one-on-one meeting with key decision-makers and secure their commitment to your issue.

8. Active in Decision-Making: Individuals or organizations who actively write or refine the bill, policy, or program that addresses your issue.

10. Decisive in Decision-Making: Individuals or organizations with the (often voting) power to give you what you want.

Figure 4: Levels of Power

You can figure out an individual's alignment on your issue by doing some research. Have they spoken on your issue previously? Have they voted on it? As with your own placement on the map, expect the placement of decision-makers to shift during your campaign, though their movement is likely to be most pronounced along the alignment axis as opposed to the power axis. In the absence of specific information, decision-makers should be left off the power map. There is a significant difference between knowing a stakeholder is neutral on an issue and not knowing where said stakeholder stands on an issue. That difference becomes obvious after revisiting a power map.

The third category of placements comprises any *other stakeholders* invested in this issue. whether allies or opponents, the organizations or individuals with the ability to influence the position of your decision-makers are crucial to recognize, as they can affect your placement in an upward or downward direction and the placement of decision-makers to the left or right on the map. These stakeholders, such as media outlets, prominent public figures, business leaders, nonprofit organizations, and school districts, can exert their influence through formal power, informal power, or both.

A Living Document:
How Actions Move Stakeholders on the Map

With all of these pieces placed, the real work of power mapping begins. An initially set power map only captures the power and alignment of stakeholders in that moment. The actions taken by the individuals and organizations on the map—from big events such as a public demonstration to minor events such as a strategic meeting with key stakeholders—will inevitably shift the placements of other stakeholders. As each one likely has different priorities and networks, actions will influence different stakeholders in different ways.

Because you ultimately wish to achieve the goal in your agenda, moving stakeholders on the map follows a general logic. Naturally, winning over every decision-maker or stakeholder on an issue is not possible. Sometimes the best that you can achieve is moving some-

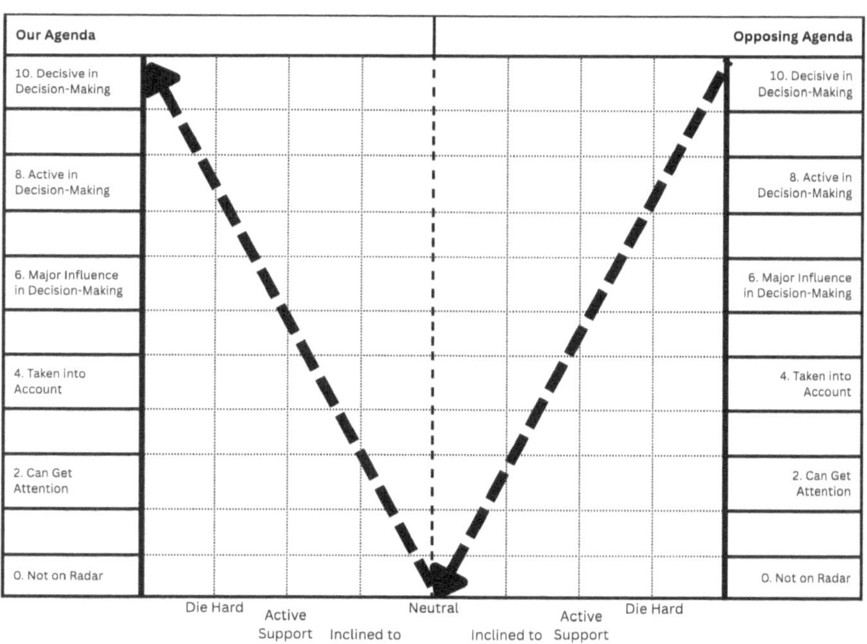

Figure 5. How Actions Move Stakeholders on a Power Map

one from die-hard opposition to a more neutral stance. As seen in
Figure 5, moving those who oppose your agenda toward a place of
lower power and/or less die-hard opposition is generally wise. For
those starting neutral or generally aligned to your agenda, the goal is
to empower them and deepen their support, ultimately landing at the
top left of the power map. While many stakeholders may fall close to
the dotted line in your own power map, remember that your goal is
to move as many stakeholders into an advantageous position as possible, whether that means weakening opposition or strengthening your
supporters. This often takes the form of bringing in stakeholders far
from the dotted line, whether they are die-hard supporters not on decision-makers' radar or powerful decision-makers who are entirely
neutral.

The Inconsistent Laws of Individual Stakeholders

As previously stated, the actions taken by any individual or group
on the map can have entirely different impacts on stakeholders' placements. An action that rallies your base and boosts your own power
may alienate neutral stakeholders and decision-makers, driving them
away from supporting your agenda. In cases like these, knowing how
you will achieve your agenda and specifically how many decision-
makers you will need to make it happen is important. Sometimes it is
strategic to alienate some decision-makers in favor of winning over
others. Other times doing so only emboldens your opposition.

To make matters worse, the different stakeholders on a power map
are not all subject to the same rules; they are people, after all. Perhaps
all you need to swing a decision-maker in your direction is to have
a specific individual or organization reach out to them. At the same
time, perhaps some decision-makers will flatly oppose your agenda
because a particular individual or group is prominently associated
with it. Politics is not known to be dominated by humble individuals,

so factoring egos into how your actions influence different stakeholders can be a frustrating but necessary exercise.

Plotting these interactions visually and over time with a power map not only makes it easier to keep track of your strategy's influence on local conditions; it also provides a broader perspective of your campaign's progression. To learn that one important stakeholder refuses to meet with you because of a personality clash with a partner may be infuriating, but if you look at your power map and see how close you are to winning or losing your agenda, you can contextualize that frustration in the broader scheme of the campaign and inform future tactics. In other words, a well-maintained power map can convey whether the frustrations rooted in one stakeholder are even worth your effort to assuage.

The lack of an overarching consistency to the stakeholders on a power map also provides an opportunity. In the same way that some stakeholders alienate other individuals or groups, other stakeholders may have an air of gravity (informal power), allowing them to pull multiple others in their direction. The stakeholders who can move multiple decision-makers simultaneously should be high priorities for you or your group as you pursue your agenda, especially if they sit in the middle of your power map. Getting these stakeholders on your side, or at least minimizing their opposition, is a significant step toward achieving your agenda and developing your own group's total power in the process.

Case Study: Revoke Town Dancing Ban

Consider the example of the fictional group Dancers United and their power map designed to revoke a town's dancing ban. The ban, enacted by the seven-member town council, has been in place for over a decade. Revoking the ban would require at minimum a 4–3 vote by the town council. Figure 6 presents the alignment of five of seven council members with regard to that agenda.

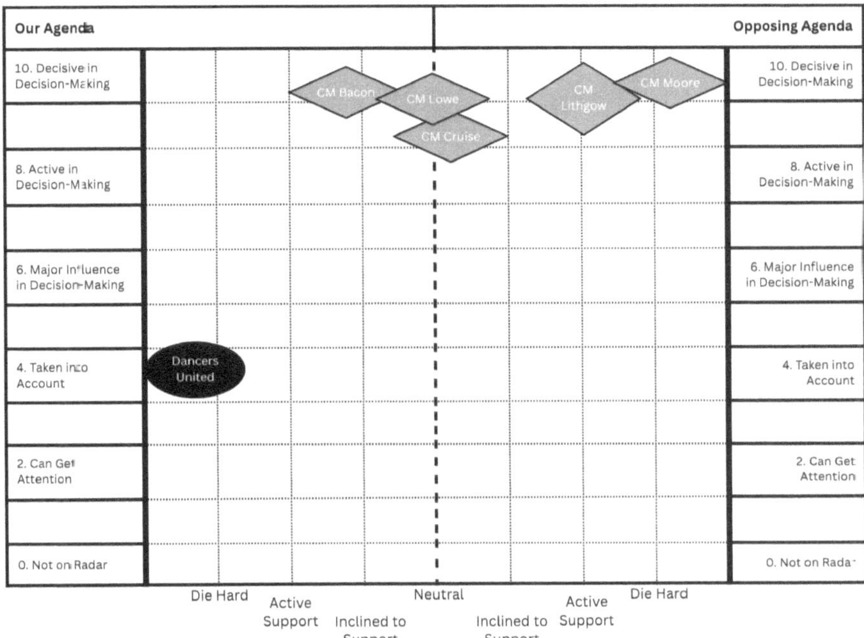

Figure 6. Case Study: Initial Power Map

Based on available information, Dancers United determined that Council Members Moore and Lithgow actively oppose revoking the dancing ban, with Council Member Moore in die-hard opposition. Meanwhile, Council Members Cruise and Lowe are generally neutral on this issue. Council Member Bacon is inclined to support revoking the ban but is not actively pushing the issue. In this iteration of the map, only five of the seven council members have been included because Dancers United was unable to find any relevant information about the last two council members.

To further complicate matters, consider the placement of other local stakeholders as shown in Figure 7. While several organizations sit around the middle of the power map, it is important to notice the Anti-Dancing League, considered slightly more powerful than Dancers United, on the complete opposite end of the power map.

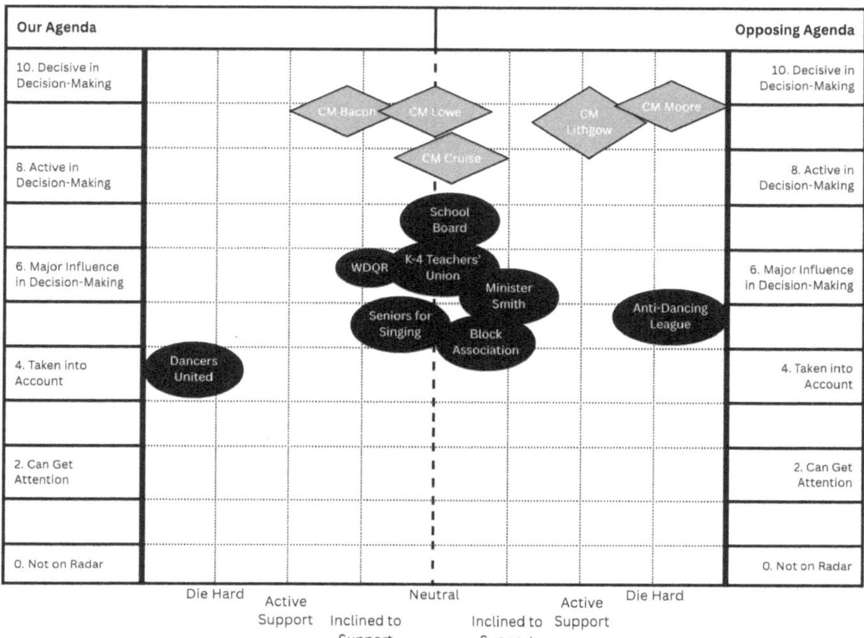

Figure 7. Case Study: Expanded Power Map

Given these placements for the local stakeholders, Dancers United can take several possible steps:

- Research the remaining two council members to determine their position on the power map.
- Begin outreach to the local groups sitting in the middle of the power map.
- Research if any other local organizations or individuals have connections with key decision-makers.
- Research the Anti-Dancing League to gain a better understanding of how they influence decision-makers and who they influence.
- Reach out to Council Members Bacon, Lowe, and Cruise to understand the strength of their neutrality.

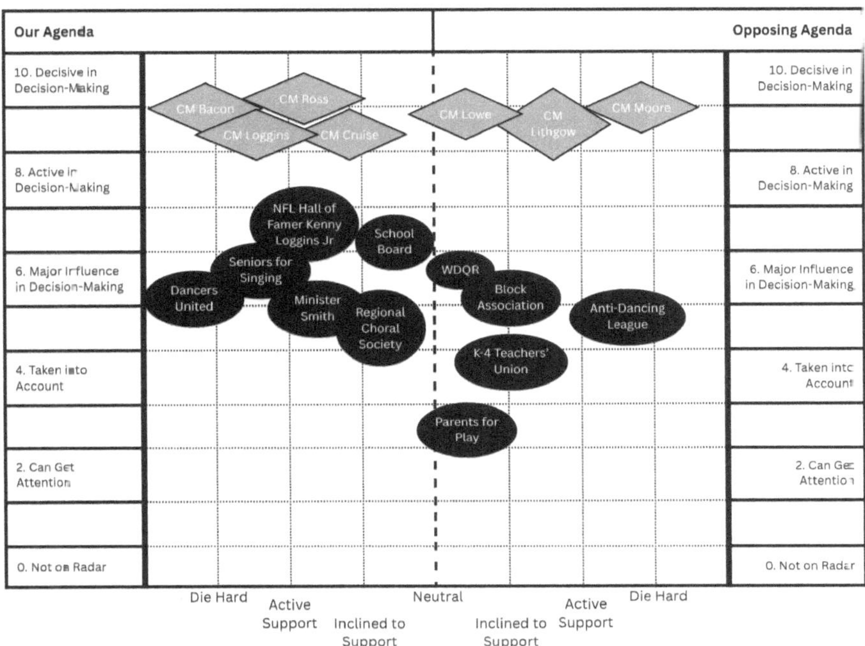

Figure 8. Case Study: Power Map End State

As they proceed with any of these steps, Dancers United may come to find that certain groups have particular affinity for, or opposition to, other stakeholders on the map. Over the course of their outreach and engagement efforts, they may learn about ways to reason with Council Members Lithgow and Moore, at least enough to minimize their opposition. Additional stakeholders may need to be added to the power map as time goes on. If the Anti-Dancing League is in fact heavily opposed to revoking the ban, they could also mobilize their opposition to Dancers United to move stakeholders in their direction.

After months of meetings, research, and public education with the various stakeholders, the power map reflects a new reality, as shown in Figure 8, where all decision-makers are placed and new groups have joined the supportive side. The most noteworthy addition to the power map is NFL Hall of Famer Kenny Loggins Jr., who credits his success in professional sports to picking up dance after graduating from the local high school. Loggins, son of Council Member Kenny Loggins Sr., made a decisive phone call to his dad after hearing about the possible revocation of the dancing ban on WDQR, a prominent local radio station. After a successful charm offensive with the considerably powerful Seniors for Singing group, the senior organization secured the support of Council Members Bacon, Ross, and Cruise. Together with the involvement of the town's favorite son and hometown hero, Dancers United secured the support of a fourth crucial vote to revoke the dancing ban.

Applied Strategy and Tactics

Of course, Dancers United could have taken several routes to achieve this successful outcome. In the case study, the absence of a prominent ally (NFL Hall of Famer Kenny Loggins Jr.) may have resulted in only three votes, one short of passing the coalition's preferred policy. Alternative routes include but are not limited to more extensive engagement with allied and neutral stakeholders, deepening the coordination with key decision-makers to win over the neutral and oppositional elected officials, or even a targeted effort to minimize the influence of the key opposition. Depending on the campaign's length of time, advocates could have also waited out oppositional decision-makers and run their own candidates in the next election to win the necessary votes to revoke the dancing ban.

Through their visual nature, power maps help to inform strategy and determine which tactics may resonate to the greatest extent. Door-knocking may galvanize your allies and win over neutral stakeholders; it also may antagonize decision-makers who prefer their constituents to remain ignorant. Understanding the nuances of individual stakeholders and how actions move them is precisely the reason why power maps are so important to crafting effective campaign strategy. (Refer to the appendix for some power mapping considerations.)

Identifying which stakeholders remain fixed over time on a power map is an equally valuable exercise once you have established your power map. Strategically, a stakeholder whose position remains consistent over months and years is unlikely to be worth trying to sway with specially crafted tactics. If the stakeholder is a vital decision-maker such as an elected official, it may be worth exploring when their term is up. If the stakeholder is just another individual or group, their placement on the map will determine whether it is best to engage them, ignore them, or work to minimize their influence on other stakeholders.

These and other questions are best addressed by the group completing the power map. While individuals can complete power maps alone, working with a group brings more perspectives on the power and alignment of stakeholders, more ideas for how to move stakeholders, and more opportunities to build community in pursuit of a shared outcome.

Review Questions

- How would you use a power map in your local endeavors? If you were to do this in a meeting, who are the people you would want to include in your first power mapping exercise?
- Would you place yourself on the power map as an individual or as part of an organization?
- How frequently would you update your power map?
- Are there any notable examples of local stakeholders who are particularly magnetic or repellent to other stakeholders? How could they influence your power mapping?

NOTES

[1] The Social Change Agency, Resources: Power Mapping Canvas. https://thesocialchangeagency.org/resources/power-mapping-canvas-campaign-resource/

THE URGENCY OF COMMUNITY

If you can't fly then run, if you can't run then walk, if you can't walk then crawl, but whatever you do you have to keep moving forward.

—DR. MARTIN LUTHER KING JR.

The rapid dismantling of the United States of America's political, economic, and social infrastructure will have ramifications for years and decades to come, necessitating a countervailing movement to either restore existing or establish new institutions. Such a movement, particularly at the level necessary to meet the present conditions, requires a resurgence of civic virtue on a history-defining scale. This assessment may be intimidating. In spite of the scope of the self-inflicted wounds we are experiencing politically, economically, and socially, a stubborn inertia may suggest today's unprecedented acts are merely headlines to digest and content to consume as part of our everyday lives. Those consumed by this mindset may think, misguidedly, "The sky has not fallen for me yet. Therefore, everyone should process everything in the same way we always have, in terms of elections, checks and balances, and, if nothing else, the moral arc of the universe bending toward justice." Such a thought ignores the extent of our crises and the human interventions that have historically and actively bent the moral arc of the universe toward justice. Furthermore, it robs each and every one of us of the agency to act in the present.

We can certainly understand why this thought holds such a firm grip, even as an increasing number of people break themselves out of its clutches. Compared to the history books many of us read growing up, we have reached an age of rolling crises. Before we can fully understand a single crisis, several more are thrust into the spotlight, only to be outshone immediately thereafter by the next scandal, failure, or disaster—an overwhelming and unrelenting torrent of bad news. To make matters worse, modern technology makes this deluge available at our fingertips at every moment. In the face of such horrors, some may find the only means of coping is to scroll through the bad news in search of something positive to replace the outrage, shock, and fear—a dopamine hit to displace the dread.

Unfortunately, breaking through the delusion of detachment can just as easily lead to despair. As mentioned, the disasters we face are all-encompassing across political, economic, and social spheres. While Parts I and II presented actionable theory and skills valuable to an aspiring organizer, advocate, and community builder, this section will center the individual undertaking these tasks under tremendous pressure. In the fact of such overwhelming political, economic, and social strife, the only way forward is for individuals to work together.

7

Building Community

Under such overwhelming systemic challenges—to say nothing about the increasing difficulties of everyday life—the most sustainable coping mechanism is to build community in your immediate surroundings. Grounding yourself in that reality—your physical location in the world—is a necessary condition to building community. While finding like-minded peers through social media and the online environment brings significant benefits, we are ultimately physical beings living in a physical world. This world and our lives within it form the basis of our identity, regardless of whether we choose to reflect or reject that identity online. We are children, parents, and spouses. We are friends, neighbors, and colleagues. Our relationships define us, and they ultimately provide the means for processing and overcoming the onslaught of despair.

For those who have yet to experience the immediate impacts of the escalating crises, it is easy, preferable even, to ignore those threats until they are immediately before your eyes—when they are no longer on your phone screen but on your street, when your corner of the world is directly impacted, when the people being impacted include people you know or you yourself. The disasters of our time are the result of decades of political, economic, and social decisions that reward this thinking and behavior. Escaping the slightest discomfort to create a bubble of calm has only made those discomforts worse and that

bubble more fragile. As we can now see, that bubble is bursting for a
lot more people.

Knowing Your Neighborhood

For those who are already seeing the impacts of these rolling
crises, it is terrifying to imagine this chaos continuing. Unfortunately,
it will. Even in the best of circumstances, reckoning with the systemic
destruction and rebuilding will mean some degree of chaos for the
foreseeable future. Finding others around you who reject the in-
evitability of the status quo, however, will provide the strength you
need to go on. It will also provide you with the camaraderie, the
mindfulness, and, crucially, the power to change that status quo.
While people may not loudly project their political beliefs in public
spaces like they do on social media, there are still ways to find like-
minded individuals or directly impacted neighbors.

For so many of us who have grown up alongside and are increasingly accustomed to the security of our screens, committing to that
search can be terrifying. We may have forgotten how to build in-person relationships or where to seek them out. In that case, political education about your neighborhood or city can be instructive. What is
its history? Who has had power over it? Does it have a representative body? A library? A food pantry? Where do formal and informal
groups meet? Being in these spaces with other people grounds you in
shared experience, whether that experience involves running a municipality, establishing programs for at-risk area families, or preparing meals for hungry neighbors.

As noted in Chapter 1, because the places where you meet these
people do not typically include your workplace or home, sociologists
refer to them as *third places*.[1] While you may only go to some of these
locations for a given meeting or program, they exist inherently for
the purposes of people coming together (see sidebar). A person who
wishes to build community needs to become a student of that commu-

nity, and particularly its third places. Through engagement of these areas, individuals committed to building community will find kindred spirits, starting with those looking for the same kind of grounded human connection.

Granted, this does not mean you should walk up to every person you see on the street, in a park, or at the library and force a conversation. For every moment of extroversion, there are plenty of times people may wish to be left alone with a book. There is no set routine for building genuine connections—no get-rich-quick scheme to being social. The best advice is simple: Be as politely observant of the places you visit and the people you see as possible.

Small Businesses as Third Places

One particular type of third place is a local small business. While the inherent activity in these places is an economic transaction—the purchase of goods or services—these venues can also be areas for genuine human interaction, community understanding, and relationship-building. Interest in common products and services can also facilitate conversations between "regulars" and staff. Cafés, barbershops, corner stores, and bars are all common examples of third places with this relational aura.

Third places are special in this way because so many different things can bring people to them: the programming, the vitally needed resources, or the other people who gather there. These spaces add vibrancy to the community because they are shared. Anyone can be there, and no single person dominates them. Most importantly, they create opportunities for chance encounters, whether between long-time friends or individuals who stumble upon a shared interest. These exchanges can ground people in communal experience tied to a place. While disinvestment in civic infrastructure and atomization of contemporary life have made third places harder to find, the foundation of community life is built upon the relationships started in these third places. If there were an equation for community, it would be as follows: *Shared Experience in Place + Relationships = Community*

Knowing Your Neighbors

Shared experience is easiest to find among your neighbors. You live in the same building or on the same block. You breathe the same air. You walk or drive on the same streets. Your tax dollars go to the same places. Without getting into any elements of partisanship, you already have various similarities with your neighbors. While you don't need to be best friends with them, knowing their names certainly helps. In times of crisis, your neighbors are quite literally the closest people to you and therefore the best positioned to respond. Whether that involves making an emergency phone call (see Chapter 8), providing equipment to deal with a basement flood, or holding on to an important delivery that arrived while you were out, neighbors can be there for you in ways few others easily can. Of course, you can also be there for them.

Knowing your neighbors is beneficial to your understanding of where you live, the issues that matter locally, and the challenges people around you are facing. In the context of our moment—our era of rolling crises—this grounding and fellowship can make living through these times more tolerable. Misery does indeed love company, so knowing that you are not alone in worrying about the safety of your streets, the funding for your schools, or the quality of your air makes it easier to not just deal with these frustrations but also change them. Not every neighbor may be ready or willing to embark on that journey with you yet, but understanding them and what matters to them will make you more empathetic, more grounded, and more liked by the people around you. Remember the lesson of informal power from Chapter 2: A well-connected neighbor can be more powerful than an elected official. Informal power not only comes from relationships of deep friendship; it also comes from relationships of mutual respect.

Critically, knowing your neighbors means your neighbors will also know you. More fully engaging in your community and with the other people in that space dispels the solitude for people living in a populated area. Successfully engaging your neighbors and not seeing them as stereotypes means they are also less likely to see you in that way. Granted, some biases will persist regardless of your best efforts: Racism, misogyny, and heteronormativity are still very real things. However, building real relationships, whether grounded in trust, respect, or an affinity to shovel snow at the same time after a snowstorm, can provide a foundation that is necessary to making that place better for yourself and your neighbors.

Knowing Your Allies

Understanding the realities of your community through the lens of your neighbors will ease the search for your allies. No person is an entirely blank slate. We all have preferences for how we wish to live, just as we all have opinions on the world around us. Those opinions are likely to vary, but if enough people with the same opinions come together, they can drive changes in their surroundings for better or for worse.

Imagine seeing families struggle to cross a busy street on their way to school. If someone started a petition to install a stop sign or traffic light, the shared frustrations of parents taking their kids to school could be mobilized to achieve an important investment in the built environment. The coordination of pedestrians could lead to new connections between parents, students, and the school. These connections could result in friendships, partnerships, or collaborations that might not otherwise have occurred. After beginning to talk to pedestrians at the crossing, gaining signatures on the petition, and getting to know people better, you could draft a power map to better understand the difficulty of implementing an improvement on the busy street. Over the course of this campaign, your neighbors might begin to share concerns about other unsafe street crossings, other concerns in the community, and ultimately other causes to organize around.

All of these activities could continue regardless of whether the initial campaign succeeded.

The scope of our crises is global, but by accomplishing changes in our immediate surroundings, we remind ourselves and our neighbors that nothing is permanent. If we cannot make a street crossing safer, we have little chance or practice of making the world as a whole more equitable or just. Finding local allies with the will to develop their skills and their sense of community alongside you is therefore critical.

As you study your community, look for local institutions facing the impacts of our rolling crises. If you're worried about education funding, sit in on a school board meeting. If you're concerned about immigrant rights, stop by your local immigrant services organization. If you're troubled by your neighbors' inability to afford groceries, volunteer at your local food bank. In any case, prepare yourself to learn about the challenges people are facing in your community. As you find concerned allies, collaborate with them to find solutions. Even if you fail to secure more education funding, prevent all racial profiling, or reduce wider poverty, at the very least, you will build connections to tackle these challenges locally.

More likely than not, you will receive some mixed results. Successes will encourage you while setbacks test your resolve, but both can teach you a lesson. Allies can help you find and appreciate such lessons and thus help you strengthen the informal power in your neighborhood. At the same time, your activities create a beacon for others to find you, get involved, and further widen your community.

Addressing Differences and Maintaining Cohesion

Of course, building community is not only a matter of finding those who agree with you. As defined in Chapter 1, community is the totality of relationships—both positive and negative—within a given geographic area. In other words, building community also means finding those who disagree with you and addressing disagreements with those who you thought agreed with you. While every organizing and advocacy effort will have a unique decision-making structure (majority rule, supermajority, unanimous consent, steering committees, etc.), successfully addressing differences of opinion is a skill set in high demand across our highly divided neighborhoods. While certain disagreements should not be glossed over, most notably those rooted in the dehumanization of individuals or communities, other kinds of disagreements are inevitable in every community. The problem occurs when these disagreements become so all-encompassing that they prevent individual community members from genuinely engaging with one another.

Unfortunately, many such differences play out in school board, town council, and other public meetings. None of these settings are particularly well equipped to resolve disagreements, both because of their inflexible structure (speaking time limits, restrictions on what can be commented on, etc.) and because of their generally public-facing audience, which makes admitting fault a matter of "losing" or letting the other side "win."

By contrast, self-organized spaces have considerably fewer restrictions, less visibility, and therefore greater opportunity for honest dialogue between people who may disagree fundamentally but also share certain interests. The same conditions make it easier for generally aligned individuals to work through uncomfortable disagreements. Organizing a space for the benefit of the community, as opposed to ensuring one "side" wins and the other loses in the form of a vote or policy, lowers the temperature and, ideally, reduces the threat to individuals' senses of personal pride.

Reaching consensus, or at the very least maintaining a sense of cohesion, requires patience and sincere trust between individuals in a community, whether in public or self-organized meetings. While challenging and very often slow, building cohesion on smaller points of agreement makes tackling larger points of disagreement easier in the future. An individual may want to advance bold proposals that would genuinely benefit their neighbors, but without the trust of the relevant stakeholders—both the community at large and relevant decision-makers—any such proposal will fail. For these reasons, more than a few organizers agree that progress must happen at "the speed of trust."[2] Only when you take the time to know your neighborhood, your neighbors, and your allies will building that trust be possible.

Review Questions

- Where are the third places in your community? How often do you visit them?
- What are the major issues in your community? Who talks about them?
- How would you determine if someone is your ally?
- How would you address disagreements between allies in your community?

NOTES

[1]Ray Oldenburg, *The Great Good Place: Cafes, Coffee Shops, Bookstores, Bars, Hair Salons, and Other Hangouts at the Heart of a Community*, 2nd ed. (Berkshire Publishing Group, 2023).

[2]Stephen M. R. Covey, *The Speed of Trust: The One Thing That Changes Everything* (Free Press, 2008).

8

Preparing Yourself

At a time when social institutions and the very foundations of human rights are being undermined, remembering that power exists through formal and informal institutions is especially important. As discussed in Chapter 2, formal power is explicit and clearly defined yet vulnerable to the kind of attack we are now living through. Formal power is also tied to one's position, whether as an elected official, a professional, or a citizen, but not to a person inherently. As a result, watching the evisceration of an established political order and a trampling of established rights means witnessing the destruction of formal power. If we only understand our power through a formal power lens, it is rightfully a time of panic and existential terror.

Informal power, on the other hand, is tied to each one of us inherently. The relationships we craft and the value we add to our communities cannot be given to other people. In this book, we have focused extensively on how to leverage our power offensively to achieve changes in the world. It is also appropriate to understand the importance of leveraging this power for our own defense. And while it is unjust that so many have needed to leverage their own informal power in ways that should otherwise be done through formal institutions of power, recall the beginning of Part II: Having power is not the same as using power. Relationships should not be inherently transactional affairs. Similarly, informal power should not be inherently built for the purposes of deployment. However, in a crisis and in a time where formal power is being actively undermined, there are limited ways we can defend ourselves. The leveraging of informal power for our defense is one such way we will explore.

Creating an Emergency Call List

Too many of our neighbors live in fear of being abducted by masked men armed with weapons of war. In the months since masked agents first appeared in our major cities, communities have rightfully taken precautions, sharing know-your-rights materials and establishing rapid response networks to alert vulnerable populations and their allies of potential abduction patrols. Such interventions are tremendously valuable mobilizations of people and resources, and we can best understand them as an additional layer of preparation on top of the precautions individuals should take. Regardless of whether they are a potential target of the recent militarization of American streets, anyone concerned about these acts should be making emergency plans. In other words, they should ensure disaster preparedness at multiple levels—individual, household, community, and beyond.

As horrific acts of violence are becoming a standard sight in American communities, you may begin to wonder how you would react if you witnessed such atrocities firsthand. If you worry about being abducted or anticipate intervening to interrupt an abduction, you will benefit from creating an emergency contact list and sharing it with your most trusted family and friends. Understanding who to list is an exercise in both logistical practicality (who is physically closest) and relational confidence (who will step in for you). To be clear, this is a list of people for those closest to you to contact; you will unlikely have the capacity and space to call more than a single person at a moment of confrontation. As such, the one person you contact must understand your list and the urgency of acting quickly. In some ways, the development of this list may closely reflect the key individuals in your community visualized on a power map, as discussed in Chapter 6.

The absence of a formalized call list makes you entirely vulnerable to the circumstances of a given moment. You will not know whether anyone will be contacted if something happens to you, and you will not know if any action will be taken to ensure your safety. Such doubts may cause you to freeze in a tense situation, but sufficient preparation can ensure you are fully present if and when such circumstances affect you. Videos abound of individuals, neighbors, and passersby standing up to protect those being disappeared, but several show instances of individuals being taken without clarity around their identities or detention location. Rather than leave your own (hopefully hypothetical) experience to chance, creating and revising a list of key contacts for your most trusted person to utilize, is a crucial form of emergency preparedness.

- *Household:* Whether family or roommates, your household includes the people closest to you. Not only do they know you and presumably know your general routine, but they can immediately vouch for you and/or provide documentation if necessary. They also likely have the best sense of other people to engage.
- *Rapid Response Network (if available):* The most remarkable current efforts of community organizing include the mobilization of volunteers to alert neighbors to any abduction patrols in the area or active abductions occurring. While no single structure exists for setting up a rapid response network, some areas have none at all. For those with an active set of volunteers, networks can quickly mobilize from a wide pool of trained responders to spread out over a given geographic area. More sophisticated response networks likely are connected to legal support and offer mutual aid resources.
- *Lawyer:* While no one is expected to have a lawyer on speed dial, conducting some basic research on the free legal resources in your area, the local bar association, or legal clinics could pro-

vide some direction on legal help to either de-escalate a situation or get support after someone is taken.

- *Neighbors:* The potential for abduction is one of several reasons why it is helpful to know your neighbors' names. Regardless of politics, it is unlikely anyone wants to see their well-known neighbor getting zip-tied and thrown in the back of an unmarked van by masked agents. A neighbor may call more attention to the situation, attempt to defuse it, or directly intervene. Not every neighbor would risk their own safety for you, but understanding what those in your neighborhood would do in the event of an abduction is vital when considering how quickly they should be contacted.
- *Colleagues:* Depending on the location of an incident, your colleagues may be the equivalent of your neighbors. Your superiors in particular may have more success in de-escalating not from a moral or political position but from an economic and business angle.
- *Allies:* Unfortunately, our strongest allies may be the hardest ones to mobilize from a logistical standpoint. Those same allies, however, could be uniquely positioned to make a big difference. Local elected officials could leverage their formal power to investigate and demand accountability. Institutional leaders could gather resources or rally individuals to action. Reporters could document injustice and elevate an incident into a broader story with regional or national ramifications.

Identifying the appropriate people for your list is not an individual exercise. Particularly because so much is at stake in these circumstances, it is important to talk with the people you plan to list to ensure you understand how much they are willing to do or not do, most importantly the first person who will initiate all of the subsequent calls. By initiating these uncomfortable but necessary conversations, you open up a dialogue around the severity of our collective situation, and you put yourself out there in the hopes that the people you speak with will stand up for you. This can feel awkward or even overly dramatic, but it is better to have these conversations and never need to test people's commitments than to never have the conversations and end up with no one ready to respond. In the best case, the people on your list will surprise you, offering other individuals or resources who could provide support or stick up for you in unexpected ways. Additionally, they may consider creating their own list and making you one of their emergency contacts, an easy multiplier effect for preparing your allies. The only way to find any of this out is to have the conversation. Especially in the heat of an abduction or confrontation, the last thing you should be thinking about is whether you included the right people on your emergency contact list.

With conversations completed, consider how to arrange the call list. You could organize the order of contacts by proximity to your location or the closeness of your relationship, or you could create entirely different lists based on general circumstances. Four different configurations for the same person are presented in Table 2. Particularly because we all have different circumstances and types of relationships with the people around us, there is no single way to set up an emergency call list. The most important consideration involves ensuring that the closest individuals to you (geographically and emotionally) are best positioned to prevent a negative outcome. (Guidelines for preparing your emergency call list are provided in the appendix.)

As with power maps, emergency call lists can best be understood as a snapshot in time. The people you contact first and the scenarios you plan around can shift from week to week. Revising your list by building it out with additional contingencies and nuances makes it easier for your friends and loved ones to manage in the event they ever need to utilize the list. It should also, of course, give you some peace of mind.

Table 2. Four Configurations of Emergency Call List

Scenario-Based Call Lists		Proximity-Based Call List	Relationship-Based Call List
Something Happens at Home	**Something Happens at Work**		
Immediate • Local rapid response network • Roommate/spouse • Neighbors 1 and 2 • Local pastor • Local school • Local friends (a 5–10-minute drive away) ***Government*** • Town councilor/mayor • County/state representatives ***Press*** • Local reporters/bloggers ***Others*** • Local friends (15+ minutes from home) Parent–Teacher Association (PTA) president • Community center contact • Local business owner	***Immediate*** • Local rapid response network • Roommate/spouse • Colleagues and boss • Legal department • Prominent work partners ***Government*** • (Dependent on connections in area of work) ***Press*** • Local reporters/bloggers ***Others*** • Local pastor • Local school • Local friends • PTA president • Community center contact • Local business owner	***Immediate*** • Local rapid response network • Roommate/spouse • Neighbors 1 and 2 • Local pastor • Local school • Local friends (a 5–10-minute drive away) • Local business owner • Community center contact ***Government*** • Town councilor/mayor • County/state representatives ***Press*** • Local reporters/bloggers ***Others*** • Local friends (15+ minutes from home) • PTA president	• Roommate/spouse • Neighbors 1 and 2 • Extended family • Local friends (a 5–10-minute drive away) • Local rapid response network • Local pastor • Local school • Local friends (15+ minutes from home) • PTA president • Community center contact • Local business owner • Local reporters/bloggers • Town councilor/mayor • County/state representatives

Understanding Your Limits

Admittedly, if you are committed enough to draft and revise an emergency call list, you likely have experienced at least a brief moment where you recognized the severity of what is happening all around us. Even if you have not personally witnessed an abduction patrol, the realization that people are rapidly mobilizing in response to these gross overreaches of executive authority may be overwhelming. Although I previously suggested that the best way to maintain sanity through such a tumultuous time is to build community, it is just as important to personally reflect on your own emotional, economic, and safety limits.

Organizing and advocacy work is never easy, but facing apathy is much less intimidating than facing masked and heavily armed agents trying to take people away. This is a terrifying time to even consider the idea of social justice, but your willingness to seek out answers to achieve this ideal demonstrates a natural affinity for empathy, kindness, and love. And while you may be successful in building community with like-minded individuals, you must also be mindful of your own comfortability in uncomfortable situations.

In the face of hostility, either from the government or from harassing individuals, bystander and upstander intervention trainings can provide you with a safe space to explore how you would respond when a person is assaulted, harassed, or, in more recent cases, detained and killed. Practicing what to do in such situations is just as important as understanding how you would personally react. Knowing whether you would retaliate, retreat, go into shock, or try to de-escalate the situation—the reactions better known as *fight, flight, freeze,* or *appease*—is important for recognizing your limits and (if you're unhappy with your initial response) potential areas for personal development. On a practical note, understanding your own reaction may inform how much detail to include in your emergency call list.

Beyond overt acts that require intervention, there is also simply broader hostility in the world, enabled, pardoned, and celebrated by those currently in power. While much of it is concentrated, monetized, and encouraged online, the possibility always exists that your actions or those of the people you work alongside will face pushback in the real world. That pushback can be subtle or overt: a casually racist comment in a public meeting or a misuse of public resources to monitor organizing activity. Such events have happened and will continue to happen as long as some people refuse to engage in honest dialogue or see the humanity of their political opposition. While attempting to build genuine relationships with the people around you is important, some people simply do not want to be reached and will be suspicious of your actions through no fault of your own. Organizing and advocacy work should be carried out with full consideration of these realities.

Ignoring the dangers and the fears is not a sustainable practice for enacting change. It is often said that bravery is not the absence of fear but the full recognition of it and a commitment to move forward anyway. Such is the case with the kind of organizing and advocacy work needed now: These efforts can be ambitious, uplifting, and even visionary, but they must not ignore the dangers and the fears that paralyze many caught up in our rolling crises. Recognizing and accepting this fear, and nevertheless choosing to forge ahead, both maintains your own well-being and creates an example for others to follow. At the same time, the spaces we create for others to organize and advocate must be responsive to these fears, lest we lose potential allies for seeming detached from reality. How you move forward, whether by honing your own tactics, mobilizing and educating your peers, or finding your own way to strengthen your community, is entirely up to you.

Review Questions

- Who would you include on your emergency call list?

- How would you approach a conversation with one of the people you include on your emergency call list?
- What is your natural reaction in tense situations: fight, flight, freeze, or appease?
- How can you create space for people to work through the real fears of our present political moment?

9

Moving Forward

In the span of less than one year, the social, political, and economic order for many residents of the United States has come undone. At the same time, it is yet to come apart for many others. For those already experiencing the unraveling, it can feel like this trend is set in stone and we are all merely an audience reacting to the latest outrage. But it does not need to be this way. The unraveling of so many systems was not predetermined a year ago, nor is it necessarily going to continue a year from now. The ramifications of recent policy decisions will absolutely be felt for generations, but, at the risk of sounding cliché, the history books of tomorrow are being written today. In the same way many of us read about the civil rights movement and the social justice warriors who fought for life, liberty, and the pursuit of happiness, our descendants will read about what we did at this moment in time—this era of masked agents abducting people, of institutional self-destruction, and of state-sponsored hostility toward the most vulnerable in our society. The story is actively being told, and we are the characters our children will learn about tomorrow.

Observed systematically, these political trends are unsustainable, particularly as more and more people feel the impact of policy decisions and push back against them. Opposing big government was once a catchy mantra, but witnessing the gutting of our public health, environmental protection, social welfare, and national transportation infrastructure is more likely to radicalize people than validate small government slogans. As the impacts continue to worsen, those who once may have championed slashing government will look for ways to get things back on track, at the very least for themselves, likely starting with the simplest task: voting.

Elections may result in a redistribution of formal power, but the evisceration of government in our time has had the secondary effect of weakening the legitimacy of that formal power. When the leader with the most formal power undermines the institutions they lead by misusing or dismantling them, that leader also weakens their formal power and the formal power of their successors. Given this recent history, putting one's full faith into the ballot box is unwise. Furthermore, a change of leadership does not necessitate an effective and complete reversal of damaging trends (see the 2020–2024 interlude).

As anyone following the changes occurring within our government or on the international scale would rightfully conclude, a single election is insufficient to address the rolling crises currently underway. The forces that have taken hold of government are organized, coordinated, and committed to their generally aligned causes. So too must the responding movement be organized, coordinated, and committed, albeit to entirely different ends. The system as a whole has been broken from the inside out, and the sooner people realize this, the sooner we can intentionally begin the multigenerational work of restoration, renovation, or revolution.

Beyond elections, neighbors have mobilized, and individuals are doing what they can—organizing and advocating in local campaigns for food and clothing collection, assembling immigration rapid response networks, and bolstering the power of local and state governments to resist the authoritarian tide. These actions and those like them build the kind of informal power necessary to challenge and undermine the illegal and illegitimate acts of those with formal power. As indicated in both the examination of the forms of power in Chapter 2 and the power mapping case study in Chapter 6, an individual or group can potentially build more power than an elected official. Short of the opposition party grinding government to a halt, accumulating informal power to meet the abuses of those with formal power seems like the only viable course for addressing the ills of our current era.

Accomplishing this effort is an enormous and collaborative endeavor. The pockets of organizing and advocacy in communities across the country are the seeds of civic virtue necessary to meet the moment. Engaging with one another instead of spiraling individually is necessary for our collective survival and our personal sanity. It also demonstrates that a different politics is possible and actively underway. Although it may not resolve all of our current rolling crises in the short term, our natural inclination to engage one another and try will ultimately result in our success. The moral arc of the universe will bend toward justice again because enough people still have the morality to see and the courage to act in the face of injustice.

Of course, talk of cosmic forces means nothing to the individuals losing access to health care, rights, or loved ones. Civic virtue lacks the nutritional value necessary to feed a family. Too many are already suffering as a direct result of this era's policy decisions. While we may win in the long term, too many today are already losing and will not live to see the victory pursued by many around the country.

This realization, both in the losses already underway and in the potential losses to come, should motivate you to act. Whether you are outraged by the countless people who have disappeared or by the realization that you are just as vulnerable as any of the abducted, the moment to plan is now. Whether you are dismayed by the growing need at our food banks or by the necessity to visit one for your family, the moment to engage your neighbors is now. And whether you worry about the future in the abstract or for the children in your own life, the moment to organize is now. With so many already suffering, no one should do so in silence.

A renewed sense of collaboration must overcome the trend toward atomization. Informal power, at its core, is built upon the basic understanding that we are social creatures. As such, it has a unique quirk: Informal power strengthens not only one person, but all those in the relationship. If a neighbor gains the trust of others as a resource on their block, that neighbor grows their own informal power and the informal power of their neighbors. We can therefore understand informal power as mutually beneficial, just like a healthy relationship.

As described in Chapter 3's discussion of the Awakening Perspective on Power, informal power is limitless. When neighbors in a community awaken such power, they have the potential to achieve purpose, to shift the formal power of a political system from oppressors to the oppressed—in other words, to realign it.

Although it may come across as simple when described in this way, the reality is that we need this sort of local coordination to achieve national mobilization. It may seem slow or meager in the face of the atrocities we are regularly experiencing, but it is the necessary work of building sustainable and sufficient power to meet the moment. Even if the ultimate goal of building community and organizing neighbors is not to address systemic injustices, that locally focused work can inspire other communities that may wish to tackle broader issues. Every community is experiencing these systemic challenges, and none has a perfect set of solutions. The best thing we can do is try, and when many people try together, they can learn from one another. This lesson applies within and across communities: Communities can and must learn from each other, but we need to build them first.

In the face of so much dramatic change over a short period of time, it is tempting to be nostalgic for a bygone era. As history demonstrates, time and people can only go in one direction. While some, including those in power right now, may wish to revert to an earlier period and are willing to sacrifice much of the country and its subsequent achievements to do so, in reality we can never go back. Even if the criminals of our present were all held accountable, we could not go back for two interconnected reasons.

The seeds of our current crises were planted, nurtured, or ignored in our past. The abuses of power today were only made possible by expanding those powers in earlier periods. And when those powers were previously abused, the failure to hold abusers accountable enabled the abuse of our present. The vicious treatment of marginalized people today builds upon the legacy of dehumanization of political opponents, virulent nationalism masquerading as patriotism, and the unwillingness of our political class to directly address the legacy of racism. The impunity of actions by our leaders was facilitated by a cowardly political opposition that convinced themselves and the general public of political norms and values that were destroyed decades earlier. Going back, in this case, means to simply rewind the clock to 30 seconds, 60 seconds, or a few minutes before midnight. While such may seem preferrable to our present predicament, it is also impossible for a second reason.

All of us have been changed through the ordeal of these times. Society cannot go back because individuals cannot go back. We have seen too much, lost too much, and experienced too much to forget the lessons of this period. The experience of COVID-19 and the general attempt to swiftly move past it demonstrates a discomfort with learning from our past. Unfortunately, we are currently facing the consequences of failing to reckon with the scope of that and other crises. So long as we allow ourselves to do so, we are always learning, reflecting, and adjusting to meet the circumstances of our daily lives. Going back is antithetical to this natural rhythm and fails to honor the experiences—including the losses—so strongly felt today. If we accept that we can learn from these experiences, we can be better than we were before.

Going backward may tempt us because it provides security: We know how we felt, how we lived, and what mattered in the past. By contrast, the future is terrifyingly uncertain. Fear of the unknown is perfectly reasonable, and as indicated in the Chapter 8 section on understanding your limits, coming to accept these fears is crucial to your own well-being. The solution to this fear, however, is not to go backward or freeze to a moment in time; instead, we must endure and go forward. As generations behind us were uncertain of the future in the face of fascism, institutionalized racism, misogyny, and planetary self-destruction, so too must we address these and other challenges without knowing the outcome. Things now are decidedly bleak, but the uncertainty of tomorrow yields possibility today. As we have seen, things can get worse, but they can also get better. Which outcome happens is dependent on the steps we take today. And while your steps may be uncertain, they will not be taken alone as thousands of others similarly try to make sense of this uncertain era. If you look around, you may even see your neighbors taking those steps in your own community.

Glossary of Terms

- **Advocacy:** The act of working on behalf of other impacted people to achieve a shared goal.
- **Advocate:** One who works on behalf of an impacted class of people to achieve improvements in their material conditions.
- **Awakening Perspective on Power:** The idea that power is inherently held by individuals and must be activated in order to achieve desired outcomes.
- **Campaigns:** A series of activities that work in service to a goal.
- **Community:** The totality of positive and negative relationships within a given area.
- **Formal power:** Power automatically given or conferred to an individual or group as a matter of professional, economic, or political position.
- **Informal power:** Power gained through camaraderie, friendship, partnership, and shared experiences.
- **Organizer:** One who works with an impacted class of people to achieve improvements in their material conditions.
- **Organizing:** The act of working alongside other impacted people to achieve a shared goal.
- **Politics:** People exerting the ability to achieve purpose over their surroundings.
- **Political education:** Learning about power and its use in communities and between people.
- **Popular education:** A way of learning that allows for an individual to actively and collaboratively learn as part of a group.

- **Power:** According to Dr. Martin Luther King Jr., "the ability to achieve purpose" and "the strength required to bring about social, political, or economic changes."
- **Praxis:** Application of theory and learning from the experience of that application.
- **Realignment Perspective on Power:** The idea that power is concentrated in certain hands and requires reapportionment in order to achieve desired outcomes.
- **Strategy:** A planned series of interconnected actions that work toward the achievement of a goal.
- **Tactics:** The individual acts that make up a strategy.
- **Total power:** The sum of the formal and informal power any one person or entity holds.

Sample Meeting Agenda

Purpose: Build community as we process recent local events and brainstorm ways to collectively respond.

Outcome: Participants will leave with new relationships and small groups formed to carry brainstormed ideas forward.

Process: The meeting will be held in-person at ABC Community Center (space acquired and donated by Commissioner Jones) from 5 to 7 p.m., with food being purchased by Dr. Ortiz and childcare being offered by Care Collective. Volunteers will arrive at 4:15 to set up space, test out the audiovisual equipment, prop the door open, ensure accessibility according to the Americans with Disabilities Act, meet the food delivery person at 4:30, and prep the sign-in table.

A. Welcome and Level Setting (10 minutes)
   A. Facilitator: T. Alker
   B. Logistics: Childcare, restrooms, and Wi-Fi
   C. Introduction: Give your name, how you heard about this meeting, and one word to describe your emotions in this moment
B. Reviewing Current Local Events (10 minutes)
   A. Speaker: Commissioner Jones
   B. PowerPoint presentation
C. Community Processing (30 minutes)
   A. In breakout groups of four or five, answer the following:
      A. What resonated most from the presentation?

      B. What should the community do in response?

      B. Have one speaker ready to share your answers with the larger group

      C. Be sure to reintroduce yourselves!

D. Group Discussion (30 minutes)

      A. Breakout Group Report-Outs

      B. Questions for Discussion

            A. What are the commonalities between the groups? What are the differences?

            B. What should the community do in response? (List the top four responses on the projector screen.)

            C. Which actions are most compelling? (Stand-Up/ Sit-Down Activity)

                  A. Why is this action most compelling to you?

                  B. What can you personally do to move this action forward?

E. Close-Out (10 minutes)

      A. Reintroductions to your neighbor

            A. Name

            B. How you are feeling right now

            C. Way to stay in touch before the next meeting

      B. Reminders

            A. Sign-in sheet

            B. Social media handles

Sample Meeting Activity

THE FOUR CORNERS OF AN EFFECTIVE CAMPAIGN (20-40 MINUTES)

Purpose: Meeting participants discuss and unpack their opinions on what makes an effective campaign.

Outcome: Participants develop a shared understanding of the different elements of an effective campaign and know how their peers consider those elements.

Process: Setup and Instructions:

- Secure a room with four corners that allows sufficient space for participants to walk around and congregate in small groups at the corners.
- Print out the following sentences (or come up with your own) and place one at each of the four corners:
    - An effective campaign is a well-executed strategy.
    - An effective campaign is successful in achieving its goal.
    - An effective campaign has space for learning and reflection.
    - An effective campaign is fun.

- Introduce the activity to participants. Everyone will have a chance to walk around the room and read each statement about an effective campaign. After reading these statements, they will be asked to pick the one that most resonates with them and stand in the appropriate corner. Once everyone selects their statement, there should be (at most) four groups. Each group will have 5–10 minutes (depending on the size of the overall group) to answer the following questions:
  - Why did you pick this statement?
  - Were you torn between this and another statement? If so, which one?
  - How can you ensure the statement you chose remains true during a campaign?
- After groups have had a chance to answer the questions, bring everyone back for a full discussion (10–20 minutes). Each corner should share what their group discussed. The full group can then answer the following questions:
  - Do these statements seem mutually exclusive? Why or why not?
  - Does the size of the group determine which statement is most true? Why or why not?
  - How can a group balance these statements during the course of a campaign?

Note: This activity can be modified in several ways, such as by changing the number of statements, the topic being discussed, the length of time for each portion, or the questions that prompt the small- and full-group discussion. If the activity cannot occur in person, it may be recast to fit a virtual setting. The most important element to retain is the opportunity for participants to engage with one another, learning through dialogue and reaching their own conclusions through the activity.

Checklist for Event Planning

Overarching Considerations

- What is the *purpose* of your event?
- What is the *outcome* of your event?
- What is the *process* for your event?

Pre-Event Considerations

- Who is the intended audience for your event?
- Do you have a team to help coordinate the event?
- Have you secured a location for the event?
    - How accessible is it (transit, parking, stairs, elevators, security, etc.)?
    - Will you need volunteers to direct people?
    - Is your location the right size for your audience?
    - Where are the restrooms?
- What is the agenda for your event?
    - Who is scheduled to speak during your event?
    - Will they deliver any presentations?
        - Do you have electricity, power cords, projectors, etc., to allow for PowerPoint presentations?
        - Do you need to review the presentations ahead of time?
    - How long will the event run?

- ▪ Does your venue close or become less accessible after a certain point?
- ▪ Do you need to include breaks?
- ▪ Will you provide refreshments?
- How will you track attendance/interest?
    - ○ Should participants register ahead of time?
    - ○ How will you promote your event?
    - ○ How will you engage your audience ahead of the event?
    - ○ How will you communicate any meeting changes to your audience?

Event Considerations

- What is the overall agenda?
    - ○ How early do you need to arrive to set up tables, chairs, and technology?
    - ○ Do you need to unlock any entrances/accessways or put up any signage?
- Do you need an alternative plan in case of inclement weather?
- Do you have an understanding of the key roles involved?
    - ○ Who is facilitating the event?
    - ○ Who is keeping track of time?
    - ○ Who is welcoming attendees?
    - ○ What other key roles might volunteers fill to support your event?
- Do you need to print any materials for attendees?
- Are guest speakers/presenters aware of the time allotted?
- What do you want participants to leave with (materials, a call to action, knowledge of the next event, etc.)?

Post-Event Considerations

- How will you collect participant feedback?

- When will you debrief with your event team?
- Who will support you with event cleanup?
- How will you follow up with participants (e.g., email, phone call, text message)?

Checklist for Public Speaking

- **Why are you talking?**
  - What is the public speaking activity (public hearing, media event, public action, meeting presentation, etc.)?
  - Can you use visual aids?
  - What do you hope to accomplish?
- **Who is your audience?**
  - Is your primary audience allied, opposed, or neutral to your position?
  - Is success contingent upon press coverage (getting quoted, interviewed, etc.)?
  - What kind of information motivates your primary audience?
  - What kind of information alienates your primary audience?
- **What will they remember?**
  - What are the key points of your remarks?
  - How will you reinforce your key points during your public speech?
  - How will you know if your remarks resonate with your primary audience?
- **What are the logistical considerations?**
  - Where are you speaking? Is a microphone or podium available, or will you need to project your voice?
  - How much time will you have to speak?

- Can people interrupt your comments? How prepared are you for interruptions?
- Are there limitations on how you deliver your remarks (e.g., related to a specific piece of legislation)?
- For public hearings, can you gain additional time by having an elected official ask a question?
- Are you permitted to bring copies of your remarks?

Considerations for Power Mapping

Initial Mapping

- What specific agenda do you want to visualize on your power map?
- Besides you, who are the relevant stakeholders for your power map?
    - Decision-makers for your agenda
    - Supporters of your agenda
    - Opponents of your agenda
    - Neutral or unaligned individuals and groups
- For initial horizontal placement, consider the following:
    - How supportive or oppositional is each stakeholder? Have they spoken publicly on your agenda?
    - Are your opponents unaligned because they choose to be or because they have not previously engaged with this issue?
    - If you have a relationship with a decision-maker, how strongly do they support your agenda? *Fair warning:* You are likely to overestimate their support.
- For initial vertical placement, consider the scoring system:
    - **0. Not on Radar:** Generally the category where any unengaged person on the street would fall.
    - **2. Can Get Attention:** Individuals or organizations who could effectively garner the attention of decision-makers.

- ◦ **4. Taken Into Account:** Individuals or organizations who could write a letter or make a phone call to a decision-maker and get a genuine response.
- ◦ **6. Major Influence in Decision-Making:** Individuals or organizations who can get a one-on-one meeting with key decision-makers and secure their commitment to your issue.
- ◦ **8. Active in Decision-Making:** Individuals or organizations who actively write or refine the bill, policy, or program that addresses your issue.
- ◦ **10. Decisive in Decision-Making:** Individuals or organizations with the (often voting) power to give you what you want.

- For coalitions advancing a complex agenda, balancing the needs of coalition partners with the desires of decision-makers may be difficult. Here again lies the value in explicitly defining your agenda and having an honest conversation about each coalition member's relationship to that agenda. To this point, mapping your coalition as a single entity implies a single position in terms of alignment and influence. If that does not accurately reflect your coalition, perhaps you should map each coalition partner individually. Such individual mapping may help to inform conversations if/when disagreements within the coalition occur.

- Never place a stakeholder on the map unless you understand their actual position on your agenda. "Neutral" and "unknown" are different positions. Particularly once stakeholders start moving, seeing neutral stakeholders dramatically shift in one direction or another could be wrongly attributed to good or bad strategy. If you do not know where a stakeholder stands, keep them off the map until you can determine their position. Such research is a great avenue for some self-guided political education.

Revising the Map During a Campaign

- Start with a single stakeholder and consider the following:
    - How have your actions and the actions of other stake-holders moved this particular stakeholder? Are they more or less aligned? Are they more or less decisive in decision-making?
- After moving one stakeholder, consider how their movement may impact adjacent stakeholders. Does this stakeholder repel others, or do they demonstrate a gravity that may pull others along?
- Repeat these steps with each stakeholder on your map.
- After seeing if and how stakeholders have shifted based on your actions, consider whether the stakeholders are generally moving in a positive (leftward and upward) or negative (rightward and upward) direction. Explore what kinds of actions caused the recently tracked movements. If they generally resulted in positive movement, the actions are worth replicating. If they resulted in stakeholders moving away from your agenda and strengthening the opposition, consider a change of tactics.
- Most likely, uniform movement will not occur in one direction or another. In these cases, understanding how to enact your agenda is especially important. If your stakeholders include only one decisive decision-maker, getting them as close as possible to the upper-left corner of the power map should be your primary goal, even if it results in losing other stakeholders. If several decision-makers are required to deliver your agenda, stay focused on how many you need. If you need only a simple majority of a legislative body to pass a bill, it is not necessarily worth courting every single legislator. Of course, you can also win over decision-makers by weakening your agenda, but be-ing explicit about your agenda at the beginning of the power

mapping process should help mitigate the diluting that often happens in policymaking spaces.

- As stakeholders move toward or away from your position, examine how your power (or the power of your coalition members as a whole) changes over the course of the campaign. While the objective is to achieve your agenda, your own growth or decline in power can indicate how well your campaign is performing. If your power is growing, you are likely closer to achieving your goal. If your power is declining, you likely have more work to do. Your power may fluctuate over the course of a campaign, but an overall upward trajectory indicates your campaign is headed in the right direction. It also serves as a visual reminder to your fellow advocates that the campaign is making progress.

Our Agenda								Opposing Agenda
10. Decisive in Decision-Making								10. Decisive in Decision-Making
8. Active in Decision-Making								8. Active in Decision-Making
6. Major Influence in Decision-Making								6. Major Influence in Decision-Making
4. Taken into Account								4. Taken into Account
2. Can Get Attention								2. Can Get Attention
0. Not on Radar								0. Not on Radar

Die Hard · Active Support · Inclined to Support · Neutral · Inclined to Support · Active Support · Die Hard

Preparing Your Emergency Call List

The following questions can serve as a means of structuring your emergency call list.

Proximity

- Who are you emotionally closest to in your life? Do you have a way of contacting them beyond using your own phone?
- Who are you physically closest to in your life? Do you have a way of contacting them beyond using your own phone?
- How much do these two groups of people overlap?
- In your daily activities, how easy is it for members of either group to reach you?

Resources

- Which institutions (school, work, library, local businesses, government buildings, churches, social service centers, etc.) are closest to you during your daily activities? How responsive would they be if something happened to you?
- Do you have local press, blogs, or social media pages? How would someone contact the reporters, bloggers, or administrators associated with these spaces if something happened to you?
- Do you have a local emergency response network?
- Do you have a local bar association?

Scenario Planning

- Do your daily activities vary enough that creating different scenario-based contact lists—for example, one to use if something happens at work and another to use if something happens at home—would be worthwhile?
- Who are the most important people on your contact list(s)? Assuming you can only make one phone call, your primary contacts will need to understand the situation, have access to your emergency contact list, and be able to start calling people. They should review your contact list(s) and discuss them with you in advance of an emergency.
- Depending on who else you include (lawyers, government officials, etc.), you may benefit from listing your contacts with a set of objectives—for example, "Locate me and connect me with a lawyer within the first 24 hours."
- Ideally, every person on your contact list should be aware that they are on it, particularly if they might get a phone call from someone they do not personally know (your partner, roommate, boss, etc.). This can create an opportunity to honestly discuss any concerns and work toward more comprehensive methods of community defense.

Recommended Readings

- Freire, Paulo. *Pedagogy of the Oppressed*, 30th anniversary ed., translated by Myra Bergman Ramos. Continuum, 2005.
- Hayes, Kelly, and Mariame Kaba. *Let This Radicalize You: Organizing and the Revolution of Reciprocal Care.* Haymarket Books, 2023.
- INCITE! Women of Color Against Violence. *The Revolution Will Not Be Funded: Beyond the Non-Profit Industrial Complex.* Duke University Press, 2017.
- Oldenburg, Ray. *The Great Good Place: Cafes, Coffee Shops, Bookstores, Bars, Hair Salons, and Other Hangouts at the Heart of a Community*, 2nd ed. Berkshire Publishing Group, 2023.
- Putnam, Robert D. *Bowling Alone: The Collapse and Revival of American Community*. Simon & Schuster, 2000.

Photo Credit: Henry Hung

Armando Moritz-Chapelliquen is a community and economic developer living at the intersection of politics, poetry, and philosophy. Having spent the entirety of his adult life in the orbit of organizing and advocacy campaigns, Armando is eager to teach the lessons he's learned from successes, failures, and surprises in the pursuit of equity and justice.

His political awakening occurred in his adolescent years, when he witnessed an elderly waiter being mocked by younger wait staff. The man, unable to understand any English, thought his coworkers were joking with him rather than insulting him. Eager to fit in and unable to understand, the man joined in on the laughter. Seeing something in that man reminded him of his grandparents and his own family's efforts to blend in, but Armando was afraid to speak up or do anything to intervene. Since that moment, he resolved to work towards a world where the elderly can rest and where differences are celebrated instead of mocked.

While he has a long way to go, Armando is grateful to the students and staff he worked alongside at the New York Public Interest Research Group (NYPIRG) for giving him a shot at creating change in the greatest city in the world. The rallies and actions organized in those years were formative to his understanding of the Awakening Perspective of Power. The first bill he pushed to the mayor's desk, the Stop Credit Checks in Employment Act, opened the door for him to work on citywide campaigns. Hired at the Association for Neighborhood & Housing Development (ANHD) to help build out the organization's economic development agenda, Armando's imposter syndrome pushed him to learn anything and everything he could to keep up with some of the brightest minds in commercial tenant advocacy and industrial policy. After securing land use protections for manufacturing jobs in New York City and establishing commercial tenant rights for small business owners, Armando led capacity building programs through the beginning of the COVID pandemic.

As he left New York and returned to the Lehigh Valley, Armando's passion for community led him to the Local Initiatives Support Corporation (LISC), where he continues to live vicariously through the transformative work of his colleagues across the country. As the Director of the National Economic Development team, he has prioritized having a shared language both within the organization and across the sector as a means of building more equitable and inclusive communities.

As someone itching to use his skills locally as well as nationally, Armando has gotten involved with various organizing efforts which led him to serving as Vice Chair of the Lehigh Valley Planning Commission and President of the Wilson Area LINCS Coalition for Families and Youth. Along with his wife and son, he's a regular at the Easton Public Market and a friend to those who love their home and simultaneously want to make it better tomorrow.

www.armando-mc.com